DRIFTWOOD PRESS

ISSUE 6.2

EDITORS

CREDITS

Independently published by *Driftwood Press*
in the United States of America.

Fonts: Satellite, Garamond, Cinzel, League Gothic,
& Merriweather.
Cover Image: Alexander Landerman
Cover Design: James McNulty & Sally Franckowiak
Magazine Design: James McNulty

Published in July 2019
ISSN Print: 2578-7195
ISSN Online: 2331-7132
ISBN-13: 978-1-949065-04-6

Please visit our website at www.driftwoodpress.net
or email us at editor@driftwoodpress.net.

Table of

Contents

The One You Love

Susan Jardaneh

Thirty-One

Your mother is Friday night trache cleaning and watching horror movies in bed. She's Saturday morning writing on her small whiteboard (I do not need a Hospice nurse) as you pour breakfast down her feeding tube. Your mom is Sunday morning morphine-patched and painting nails with the Hospice nurse. You take your father to church. Your father sits in the third pew from the back in the middle every time. Every time he folds his hands in front of him when everyone stands and sings. Every time he'll want to leave right after communion, saying that God will understand, and it's only then you understand how your father equates faith with consistency. You look for comfort during the homily, but the priest is in his purple that reminds you of Prince and you remember how that used to make you blush. The purple-robed priest tells Lazarus' story, the one where Lazarus' sisters come to Jesus and say, The one you love is ill. Jesus has power over death, is what the priest wants you to know. He's already died for us all. Your father stops tapping at the brown spots on his hand.

Jesus knew your mother was ill long before you did, you're thinking. Jesus said nothing. You're sure there were hints and clues, but you had other things on your mind. So it was the doctor who finally had to come and say to you, The one you love is ill. Then you had to go and say, The one you love is ill to your father, and it took a few times—more than a few—until he nodded after you spoke. The church is a carnival of stained glass and high ceilings with crosses etched on the cylindrical lights. Jesus hangs in a white sheet around his waist on a ten-foot cross. His chiseled arms and sculpted legs have your gaze until you note the nails piercing his hands and feet and the small trickle of red below his crown of thorns. It's not a come-to-me-and-lay-down-your-burdens Jesus.

The priest talks about following where the Holy Spirit will take you, but the little boy in the row in front of you turning around and aiming his finger-shaped gun at people consumes all your attention. In one wrist-flick he shoots two old ladies in floral-print dresses and a bald man wearing shorts. He has captured the attention, or maybe fear, of everyone sitting behind him, and you glance at your dad with a smile and a giggle, but he does not return either. The boy raises his thumb and index finger, aiming at the church lights. He has no knowledge of the faith demanded to carry the belief of death as not dying. He moves his finger-gun upward and aims for the ten-foot cross where Jesus hangs because no one has yet come to him and said, The one you love is ill. It makes no difference to you if the boy shoots Jesus because when you go home, Jesus will not meet you to say that your mother will rise again. Sunday afternoons mean card games rather than resurrection, and your sister who lives an hour away will come over and insist she doesn't mind the drive, same as every Sunday. Last Sunday she came over for wig shopping, but this Sunday she'll bring a framed picture of all three of you in long pink wigs and leave it on your mother's nightstand and your mother will take it out of the nightstand drawer Sunday mornings before your sister comes over. Sunday evening is for talking about your sister's upcoming wedding while your dad pours your mom's dinner through the feeding tube.

A shush of bangs echo from the boy throughout the pews, and he's firing off his finger-gun at the crucified Jesus. Be like little children, you're thinking, but you can't imagine this is what Jesus had in mind. You wonder if it makes Jesus sad, the boy slaughtering people in church, while the purpled-robed priest says that as a result of raising Lazarus, people put their faith in Jesus. People believed. The boy's mother is trying to contain her little gun-slinger, but he turns around to you. He aims his finger for your chest, and you're feeling the weight of your mother's face in your hands when you said, "Yes, hospice is for those with six months or less to live." Your knees buckle, but it is your father who is quick on the draw. Your dad's index finger is straight. He lowers his thumb before the boy can react. The finger-slinger slumps in his pew. Your father blows the tip of his index finger and wraps his arm around you.

Twenty-Six

"She's just sad," your dad says at the Red Lobster after church one Saturday evening, "and she's had these headaches, that's why she keeps in her room all the time." "It's not normal," you say. "But a twenty-six-year-old with purple hair isn't normal, either," your father says, and you fling your hair off your shoulder. "What's normal?" your dad says, and what's the comeback for that, you want to know. "Your mother is fine. She's been like this before. We support her. We pray for her. We love her as much as we can." Your father has asked the church to pray for your mother because the more people praying, the better. "So God can't hear unless a congregation of people are praying to him?" you ask. "Please," your father says. "Let's not pretend God isn't good just because the going gets tough. You don't have parents who raised you like that." You raise your fork to argue a point but can't, so the point of the raised fork shifts to ask how much can we love her. But you're afraid your father has an answer to that question, so you use your fork for your crab cake. You want to have your sister talk to your dad because she's the one who takes no prisoners and will say the smoking and drinking and pills are what is not normal and she needs to go to a real doctor who won't just give out pills like candy. But you're the daughter who is your dad's buddy, and buddies don't get each other upset. "She's already back at work," your dad says, picking up on a conversation that you haven't started. "We have survived nearly thirty years of marriage. We can survive this?" your father says. You have to smile and nod because you know their marriage has survived because your father just wants everyone to be happy. He has smiled and nodded through his marriage and you have inherited the smile-and-nod way to deal with confrontation until now because it's not making anything go away. When you watch him at church kneeled in the pew with his fingers laced together and his thumbs rubbing his temples, you understand the rigor of happy. You tell your boyfriend that you go to church because it makes your dad happy, but you look forward to the homily because it's nice to hear that God is love and wants love and no one is more important than anyone else and God put others through struggles because of His love, but, honestly, that part is still a little muddy for you. At the end of the mass, you like the part where your dad is beaming as he says hi to the other church people and introduces you again. The parishioners always shake your hand or kiss your cheek because it's a nice scene—that of you and your dad going to church and having faith.

You ride back to your parents' house with your dad in silence. You find your mother is reading in the sunroom with Enya playing throughout the house. She doesn't get up from her chair and doesn't want any food from the restaurant and doesn't look at you at first because who you spend time with has become a competition and your mom is losing. The sunlight catches the angels hanging from the ceiling so the illumination makes you unsure if they are real. You water all the plants in the sunroom before going back home and notice the small brown clay cross you made in Sunday school when you were five-years-old out of storage and now hanging on the wall. "Why now?" you ask your mother, and she matches with, "Why not now?" "It's not even a real cross," you say, "I mean, it's got flowers all over it." Your mother takes the cross off the wall and rubs her finger over the flowers. "Seems real to me. Just because it didn't come from a church and have holy water sprinkled over it by some man wearing a collar doesn't mean it's not real." You say you know, but your mother says you don't know. "How can you know," she says, "with all the church going your father has you doing?" You want to say she doesn't understand but she just might. You try to make a date to watch the Miss America pageant with her in a couple of weeks. Your mother sighs. She says okay, adding, "It's all really changed, hasn't it?" Things change, you say, but with a little effort you and her can still shake out a good time together. You hang the cross back up on the wall and ask, "How can a cross made by a kindergartener help now?" Your mother cups your chin and says, "Because it reminds me that God is love." You feel the bones in her back when you hug her goodbye. Your dad walks you out and tells you if she loses two more pounds, she's going to the emergency room.

Twenty-One

You do laundry at your parents' house in the afternoon because they're both at work and you work nights at the restaurant. Two in the afternoon on a Wednesday, you're driving to your parents' subdivision, just passing a school zone while your mom's car coasts along in the opposite direction, just about to pass your car. She's smoking a cigarette and singing and she glides right by you with her arm out the window, so close you can hear Def Leppard in her car. She doesn't give so much as a horn beep or a head nod or a queen wave, like she used to give you when saying goodbye. You call your boyfriend and he says she's just playing hooky. "Everyone's allowed," he says. "Even old people." But your mother is taking medicine now; that's about all you know because your dad said that's all there was to it: pills that are supposed to help the mood swings, the not getting out of bed for days, the shutting her bedroom door to everyone each night after five PM. You start to call your dad but stop. You drive to the school where she's a teacher's aide, but your mother's car is absent. You call your sister who's out of state and leave a message that she should call her mother soon because she's the only mother she has and one day she won't have her. Then you make another call and apologize for sounding like your dad on the first call and say that it's national Make-A-Weird-Phone-Call Day, so reach out and touch the ones you love.

You drive around town, trying to spot your mother's car again. You try to think of her favorite places to go, but can only come up with work and the grocery store. You end up back at your parents' house and find your mother's car in the driveway. Oprah is muted on the TV in the sunroom and Def Leppard is blazing throughout the house. Your mother screams, Pour some sugar on me in the name of love, and it's the image of your mother wanting anyone to pour sugar on her in the name of love that gives you a shiver. You put your laundry in and think this is a perfect time to bring in your boyfriend's laundry from the car, but instead, the kitchen table catches your eye. A mound of toy Appaloosa horses and tiaras cover the table. "Garage sales," your mother says, coming to the table. "I'm a collector now. I got all those tiaras for ten bucks and they are original Miss America tiaras from real contestants and one belongs to Lee Meriwether." "Mother," you say. "Mother," she says back. "Your turn," she says again. You're going to bring up this afternoon, because now you're kind of pissed off that your mother is the weird one when at twenty-one you are supposed to be the weird one. You follow her into the sunroom and she turns up Def Leppard again. There are angels everywhere in the room: lounging on tables, swinging from the ceiling, pictured on the walls, relaxing on the floor, between books on the bookshelves, on the TV stand. "It's my own angel network," your mother says, and she points at the TV where there is a commercial with a man dressed up as a taco, but you guess she is referring more to Oprah. Your mother starts dancing to Def Leppard's "Hysteria" and it's then you notice the tile floor is covered in dirt. Dirt from all the sunroom planters that have been dumped and are now filled with angels. "Doing some spring cleaning," your mother says. You can see Oprah's lips moving and your fear has turned into something that makes you desperate to hear Oprah. Your mother tips a small potted plant with a flick of her wrist, like spilling a drink. "Plants give oxygen, but angels can save you," she says. "Well, you might keep the plant. People need oxygen more than angels," you say. "Is that right," your mom says.

Sixteen

"Torn between two lovers," your mother sings and raises her finger, wagging it side to side like she's leading a children's sing-along. "Loving both is breaking all the rules." Your mother is stretched out, smoking on the sofa bed while watching the Miss America pageant in the sunroom. They are not lovers, really, you explain, but boys who work at the same buffet restaurant as you. You sit on one side of her, her ashtray is on the other, and the blue thermos is on the end table along with a legal pad of paper. The one boy who has a clump of coal-colored hair and a seriously slanted nose likes you, and the one with the beach-ball-bingo-prom-king face and the my-children-are-going-to-find-his-name-on-every-page-of-my-diary-dreamy eyes is the one you like. Your mother has the cure for a sixteen-year-old's lovesickness, she sure does, she says, and reaches for the legal pad and plops it in your lap. You work your work shoes off and pick at the gravy stain on your pancake-tan work shirt while future Miss Americas walk in their evening gowns and high heels and are asked to tell a little something about themselves—because a little is all they know about themselves, your mother says. You review the legal pad. You and your mother always rank the contestants to demonstrate how it should have been done. Traditionally, the highest points go to the girl with the slightly crooked teeth or the red hair or the one who does a dramatic reading or the one who uses three syllable words, but now you look at how perfect Miss Texas is with her blonde hair and you wonder if you've been living in Bizarro World. Your mother asks, "What was it like?" and you ask, "What was what like?" and she says, "The kiss that you must have had from one of these boys." "Like someone put an oyster at the end of a rubber band and shot it into my mouth," you say. Miss Florida walks up to the mike and you always put her on the list as the hometown favorite, but she's wearing a cross around her neck, so before she can speak, your mother scratches a line through her name. "The one who likes me kissed me," you say. You erase the scratched-out Miss Florida and write her back on the list. Your mother takes your pencil but you take out the cross necklace from your shirt and remind her. "You're just mad Dad is helping with Sunday school and is gone all morning on Sunday," you say. "Fine," your mother says and hands you back your pencil. "How about this Sunday I'll skip church and we can make pancakes and talk boys," you say. Your mother claps and smiles like a schoolgirl. "It gets better," your mother says and you ask, "What does?" "Everything," she says, "but the kissing will also get better." "Well, I really just let him because I thought we could get it all over with, but when it was done he had this weird look, and he said he's been wanting to do that for a long time, and I knew exactly what he meant but just about someone else." A few cigarette ashes drift onto the bed sheets and your mother doesn't notice, so you pat them out with your hand. "Even the losers get lucky sometimes," your mother sings.

Eleven

Your mother is not ugly. She is maple syrup thick, sunshine behind a building, caramel popcorn tan. You mother is Friday night pizza, Saturday morning cartoons. She is Sunday morning spiritual, Monday calling-in-well day. You make lunch. Peanut butter and potato chips sandwiches. Your mother swoons. You spend the afternoon in lounge chairs. You without a top running through sprinklers, just the cross necklace your father got you for completing Sunday school bouncing as you run. Your mother without a top, drinking from a blue thermos. Fleetwood Mac tapes saying, "Go your own way." She looks at your cross necklace and gets out her Tarot cards. You run the cross back and forth on the chain and remember it was the Lazarus story that you told your father as proof of you having learned something in Sunday school. Your mother gets out her Tarot cards, lays your future out. "Everything's coming up roses," your mother says, pouring you lemonade in a champagne glass. "Death really isn't death," you had told your father while driving back from church. And you showed him the butterfly you made in Sunday school to bring the point home that death is new life. "And that means maybe Stella will come back," you said. Your father grimaced and said he didn't think that the Lazarus story applied to goldfish, which made you a little sad and confused. But you squeal when you mother turns over the lover's card because, to you, love always means love. Your mother cups your chin. Then your father slams the front door. "Party's over, Kiddo," mother says, and closes the Tarot card book. Your father says to play next door. "But dad," you say. "But nothing," he says. "Sally's parents are having you for dinner," your father says, and your mother laughs and asks how you'll be cooked. He tells your mother to put on some clothes and hands you a shirt. Your mother snatches up your future without reading it.

Both Conscious and Unconscious

A Conversation with Susan Jardaneh

The following conversation was conducted by managing fiction editor James McNulty and fiction editor Dan Leach.

James McNulty: Hey, Susan! Congratulations on winning our first In-House contest! All our editors love this story; it received the rare unanimous rating!

Susan Jardaneh: Thanks, James. I was really surprised and excited to get the news.

JM: Let's start with the most obvious question: how'd you come to decide on the structure of the story—moving across the illness in reverse?

SJ: I was kind of in a writing rut when I started this story. I had not written for some time, but I was at a writer's conference specifically to force me back into the practice. I had the idea of using the second person perspective pretty early on with this story because I hadn't tried it before. I was also going back to some authors that are go-to writers for me and I came back to Lorrie Moore's *Self-Help* and particularly "How to Talk to Your Mother (Notes)" and really liked how the story moved backwards. I have always been interested in different structures and wanted to give one a try. I had this big issue of a mother dying that I knew conveyed lots of emotions, but I also didn't want to get bogged down in the emotions, so I thought that giving glimpses about the progression of the illness would help keep me and the story focused.

JM: I see the Lorrie Moore influence, now that you mention it. A fiction writer in our last issue spoke about climbing out of a writing rut, too. What was it exactly that helped you climb out? Reading over your favorite writers for inspiration was enough?

SJ: No, I wish inspiration just came from reading favorite writers! I think it was really getting in a community of writers, whatever that community looks like. When I started the story, I was in living in Florida and went to a residency called The Atlantic Center for the Arts in New Smyrna Beach where the Master Artist was Victoria Redel. So not only was I having to produce work, but I was also talking with writers and getting to read their work. I drafted the story at the residency, but then it was back to life and the story just sat. It wasn't until I recently moved to Oregon and got into another writers' group that I picked up the story again. There's something electric that happens, at least for me, when writers gather and talk about stories and the making of stories. There is also a good sense of accountability when you are in a writing group because they are expecting you to produce something.

JM: What changed when you tackled the story anew? Fill us in on the path this story took from creation to completion.

SJ: What seemed to change the most was my perspective on the story. The structure came pretty early on in the story as well as the voice, but then I found I had a lot of generalizations in terms of what a family dealing with a terminal illness would go through. So I had to individualize this family and their particular situation. I developed the differences in religion for the family and the idea that this narrator is being pulled between the two parents. How people handle grief is something I tried to get more particular with when I came back to the story. And it wasn't until I came back to the story that the whole ending scene came for me. When I got to know the characters better in dealing with this situation, the ending came really automatically.

JM: Children dealing with grief while navigating the pull between parental figures representing different types of being—sounds like Terrence Malick's *Tree of Life*. You mentioned the risk of "getting bogged down in emotion" earlier. On a craft-level, could you attempt to explain how you avoided sentimentality and this "bogging down"? Of course, you've explained some of it above—avoiding generalizations and landing more on the specific.

SJ: Yeah, dealing with emotions can be tricky because having too much sentimentality is such a fine line to walk. For me, it goes back to the fundamentals of showing and telling. I try to show an action or reaction, even something as small as a gesture or movement to indicate emotions as it seems much more gripping than for the writing to tell me the emotion. I'd rather feel the emotion than be told about it. I also like developing scenes and having the tension be created out of the contrast, such as contrast between what is being said and what is going on in the scene or what the author is thinking and doing, so emotion is evoked more organically and powerfully and the characters end up becoming more in charge of the story.

JM: I think that hits the nail on the head. *Showing* the emotion will always be so much stronger than *telling* it, and that strength undermines the too-overt force of sentimentality so long as your gesture isn't giving into the sentimentality in other ways, such as clichés. Much of the rest of what you said, I think, comes down to adding *subtext* to the scenes; focusing on the contrast is a great way to approach subtext.

Many writers often claim they "let the characters take charge of the story," but I'm curious what that means to you specifically. The plot arises from a solid conception of the characters and their desires? Can you pin-point exactly what you mean when you say the characters become "in charge"?

SJ: Yes, subtext is so important and so difficult to explain or teach. So, I think it means that instead of becoming more in charge of what goes on in your story, the trick is to become less in charge. I think the plot rises from a spark of the story for the author, the initial idea of the story. But then it's after the initial draft of the story where the writing really comes for me. The rewriting is where I can start to become more unconscious of how I wanted the story to be and more conscious of what the story wants to be, and that is because the characters and situations become more real and tangible. For me, the trick is not to fall into the trap of how a character in a specific situation is supposed to act or react, but how *this particular character* would act and react. So then the characters become more in charge. So, for the original ending, the mother and narrator were just outside with the sprinklers on and the mother was going to read the Love card in the Tarot for the narrator. But then going back to it, I wanted to set the scene more, so the narrator has her top off and by then I knew the mother more, so of course she has her top off too! By then I knew the tension between the parents, so the father had to come back in. And the father doesn't know how to communicate with his wife, so he uses his daughter to change the situation. And the mother's last act is one of thinking of herself as she sweeps up the Tarot cards without consideration of her daughter. But I didn't know any of this until I was less focused on what I wanted from the story initially and more focused on where the story itself wanted to go.

JM: I'm not sure I understand the dichotomy you've set up here between being "in charge" and "less in charge." Once you discover who your characters are (be it through an outline or a messy first draft), the writing becomes easier because you understand how they'd specifically react to situations, but I'm not sure that makes the writer any "less in charge." Rather, they just have a better sense of what they're doing because they understand their characters (which to some degree makes them even *more in charge*). Am I understanding that correctly?

SJ: Sure, and "in charge" isn't probably the most fitting phrasing. I guess I'm saying that knowing characters, like knowing people in real life, is a process, and even if you understand the characters after a first draft, at least for me, I still have a lot more to learn about them. And maybe what is more appropriate is how creating characters is a product of conscious and unconscious writing. I consciously know things about the characters as I'm beginning a story, but it's not until the rewriting where I can let the situation of the story really run its course and then see what this character would do. In this way, I'm really more focused on the world of the story—how it works and how the people in it act and react, rather than basing the characters' reaction on how I know people should or would react.

JM: Sounds right to me. Our editor, Dan Leach, has a few questions he'd like to ask, too.

Dan Leach: Speaking of your ending, it's been our experience that one of the hardest feats to accomplish in literary short fiction is an ending that both resolves and creates tension, one that paradoxically feels surprising and inevitable. An ending, in other words, like yours. What tips can you offer to other literary writers with respect to ending a story?

SJ: Yeah, the ending surprise me in how it turned out. I was feeling a little lost about it initially, so I wanted to get out of the story quickly and without a lot of explaining. In an ending, I think not really explaining a lot is a good way to go. So I try to focus on actions at the ending and looking back at what details have been set up previously in the story that can be brought back full circle for the ending. I also think that once you have an ending looking at the paragraph above and seeing if that could be the ending is a good strategy to help avoid over-writing an ending.

JM: All good advice.

DL: Physical and emotional intimacy seemed vital to both the voice and the theme of your story. And in terms of cultivating that intimacy through your writing, it seemed that you leveraged second-person POV in order to close the distance between the reader and the protagonist. Can you talk a little about this decision? Why second as opposed to first or even a close third, both of which also offer a sense of closeness?

SJ: I've always liked the second person, but I have never written a story in it, so the idea to try something new, especially when I hadn't been writing, appealed to me. I usually write in first person as I like the intimacy it holds, but I didn't want to be close to this situation. The subjects of religion and illness in the family are ones that many people deal with and I've dealt with also, so I didn't want my experiences taking over the story, yet I did want a closeness to the narrator where readers can feel something for her. So the second person was really an automatic choice for the story and one of the first decisions made.

DL: Several readers identified your writing as "regional" (read: Southern). Do you embrace this qualifier as writers like Ron Rash or Jesmyn Ward have? Or do you aim to reject/complicate it, such as Richard Ford or Jason Isbell?

SJ: Oh, I've lived most of my life in Florida, so some might not consider that the South, but I would be flattered to be considered a Southern writer. I'm also an admirer of both of the writers you've mentioned as well as Flannery O'Connor, Dorothy Allison, and Randall Kenan, just to name a few. I don't think about it consciously as I write, but what I write about is shaped by where I have come from and experiences from living in Florida.

JM: I've lived most of my life in Florida, too—first

Pompano Beach, then Tampa, then back to the Miami area for work. Where in Florida have you lived, and are you able to put your finger on the ways its shaped your writing?

SJ: I grew up in Daytona Beach and moved around that area a lot. I then moved to Orlando as an adult and commuted back and forth a bit before settling in a town near Orlando called Oviedo. In my writing I'm interested in how places shape people and with the great diversity of people and environments in Orlando, it's been a great place to get inspiration. It's a community full of voices and contrasts and history. People usually have their own preconceptions about Daytona and Orlando, based on the theme parks, the heat, the traffic, and the number of alligators in someone's yard that they have seen on the news, so those things provide a great platform from which to develop stories.

DL: We absolutely loved how you weaved humor into such a heartbreaking premise and such a brutally honest voice. Although the piece's primary tone is heavy and even existential, scenes like the Dad finger-shooting the kid in church or the Mom singing "Pour Some Sugar On Me" are laugh-out-loud hilarious. Aside from its obvious uses (relief, tonal variety, entertainment), what spaces does humor open up in your work?

SJ: I'm really happy to have you say that because I think humor is such a tricky thing for me to do in writing because I'm never sure how it will come off for readers. I like the idea of reversing expectations in stories, mainly because it's the way life works too—often things happen in life that we don't expect. And humor is a great tool to make characters more complex and situations more identifiable.

DL: One of the most common complaints from *Driftwood*'s editorial staff is how few writers we see making use of long, robust, multifaceted paragraphs. As I'm sure you know, the gimmicky, gut-punch short paragraph is very much in vogue these days. Naturally, we loved the risks you took in writing paragraphs that often exceeded a page. Tell us a little about your thought process in knowing when a paragraph should end. Maybe talk about what keeps you open to longer, more complex paragraphs in a literary culture that often seems to model itself after the 140-character tweet.

JM: Gosh, yes. You've summed up my usual rant very concisely, Dan. I always feel like an old man when I make that argument, so thank you for doing it for me.

SJ: Well, honestly, I think it really has to do with the desire to get writing again. In the initial drafts I was just trying to get some shape of a story down. And I think this story particularity lends itself to longer paragraphs because of how it's sectioned by the age of the narrator and how the dialogue presents itself. I think it's important to know what a particular story needs, even if it's going against a present trend. The trends in writing have a good function and can act as a great springboard. I mean, I started this story after modeling it from a Lorrie Moore story, but at some point, I had to think about what my story needed in terms of structure rather than sticking to the model or trend. At least for me, I have keep experimenting with structure and styles and voice so that I'm pushing my writing the most I can.

DL: Can we talk about this paragraph that everyone here adored: "Your mother is not ugly. She is maple syrup thick, sunshine behind a building, caramel popcorn tan. You mother is Friday night pizza, Saturday morning cartoons. She is Sunday morning spiritual, Monday calling-in-well day." In addition to the radiant syntax and razor-sharp diction here, there's a real music at work. Passages like these call to mind writers like Sandra Cisneros or Annie Dillard, whose rhythmic sentences tend to blur the lines between prose and poetry. How have you tuned your ear for this kind of language?

SJ: Thanks so much for pointing out that paragraph. The short answer is really reading. In reading and in re-reading. Along with those authors you've mentioned I've gone back to authors like Junot Diaz, Z.Z Packer, Aimee Bender, and George Saunders, along with reading other forms of writing, especially poetry and flash fiction. I've always liked this idea of rhythm in language and also love to play with it because music can have so much variation. I like to keep my stories moving and this rhythmic movement is also a great way for me to build tension in a story.

JM: So music serves as an inspiration? Any specific genre, singers, or bands? Do any other artforms inspire your work?

SJ: More than any specific kind of music that acts as an inspiration, the ability of music to change rhythms and moods in a single work is something I think of, especially with a form like a short story. I'm not sure I have any favorites as I'll listen to anything from Indie to Pop to Jazz, and I currently really like classical and instrumental music while I'm writing. But I have two younger children and they have taken over my current music selection, so I'm hearing a lot of Barenaked Ladies kids' albums and the Beatles right now.

JM: As many of our readers probably know by now, all *Driftwood* fiction goes through several rounds of comprehensive line-edits. We believe in polishing our fiction to its utmost potential. Could you talk a bit about the process of working through revisions with *Driftwood Press*? Most magazines accept stories "as-is" with little one-on-one work with the writer. Does having an editor or two take a close look at the story benefit the writing and the writer, in your view?

SJ: Yeah, this was a new experience for me and I think it turned out great. I'm a big revision person, so I was excited to make the story better and tighter but I didn't really know the process would be so extensive. It's also not often that writers get the opportunity to have such great insight on their story, so I think this was a wonderful experience and I can't see how the process couldn't benefit the writing and the writer. I first thought the revision would be just about wording and some sentences structure changes and maybe a couple of instances where the story could have stronger characterization, but the comments from the editors really challenged me to think about the voice and language of the story and how the tension develops and why. I had to think about the story in different ways, and in doing so, the story got sharper and more consistent. I really appreciated the time and care the editors took with the story.

JM: Two quick questions I tend to like to wrap up with. Where can readers find more of your work, and what are you working on now?

SJ: Well, this story is really the first after taking a bit of a writing break, so unfortunately, there isn't anything coming out soon. But I'm hoping this is a start of more of my work being published. I've just finished a collection of short stories titled *Disasters in Loveland* and hope to be sending it out soon.

JM: It's been a pleasure speaking with you, Susan. I think we've really covered some good ground here. Is there anything else you'd like to tell us about "The One You Love"?

SJ: I've had a great time. Thanks so very much. I just hope readers enjoy the story.

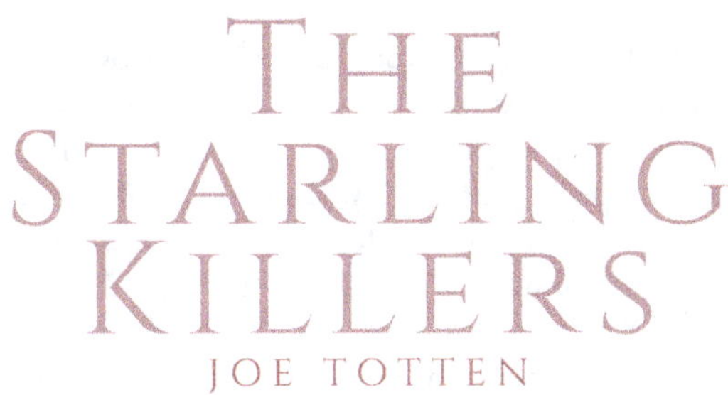

The Starling Killers

JOE TOTTEN

Randall Strayhorn focused on the amphitheater of sky displayed across the windshield of the moving truck. The morning light was just beginning to fill the immense bowl of air. A line of clouds sitting on the horizon, now in the growing light, turned out to be a distant mountain range. Strayhorn cranked down the window and put his head into the rushing air. The smell of fresh dirt, cut grass, and motor oil filled his lungs. He had a habit of constantly adjusting the vehicle's knobs and buttons; it was either too hot or too cold, the seat too far from the wheel, the radio on the wrong station or too loud. He yelled something to the boy sitting beside him and the wind carried it away. Strayhorn pulled his head back inside the cab and guided the truck abruptly into the grass at the side of the road. The dry stalks scratched at the underside of the truck. He killed the engine and was out of the cab and through the wire fence before the boy looked up.

"Bring the camera," Strayhorn shouted.

The boy had been asleep against the door and his father's shouting pulled him back from a dream. He opened the door and stepped into the grass. The noise above his head was like rushing water, a raspy exhale, loud and constant, out of place in the morning air. He knew what it was without looking up but he did anyway. An army of birds, long strings of black starlings rowed hard against the air as though reeled back into a spool. Dark moving clusters of birds, black creatures, little more than smudges of feathers, flew above his head. Hundreds of thousands of starlings spewed a dense, high-pitched scream. The boy watched the bird armada flying straight toward a grove of trees.

He followed the old man across the pasture and into the trees. Above his head the canopies met like shaking hands. It was still cool and dark under the branches. The boy couldn't see Strayhorn; his eyes were still adjusting to the dark. He moved slowly under the branches, listening to the trees breathing. The birds were settling into their roost, folding and re-folding their wings. The starlings hissed and whispered, opening their beaks to exhale or to snap a warning at another bird, grooming their feathers, jostling to find just the right spot in the trees. The sun was above the treeline now and the boy could see the birds sharply outlined by the light. Every branch was moving as if the tree had sprouted birds instead of leaves. Every limb, every branch was occupied by starlings clinging to the trees by their black, wiry talons. If the starlings had suddenly opened their wings and carried the forest into the sky, the boy would not have been surprised.

The smell under the trees was a ripe mix of salt and rotten eggs, a sweaty funk of birdshit and dust and feathers. The droppings fell like a light rain. The boy turned to go back to the truck when he saw Strayhorn standing in the field just beyond the edge of the trees. The old man was waving at him.

Randall Strayhorn had gray tufts of hair sprouting out of his ears and nose. Thick eyebrows arched off his forehead like the plumes of a tropical bird. His focus was birds and all other details in his life orbited that central idea. He was average height but his arms were long for his body, so as he walked, he leaned forward to keep pace with the momentum of his swinging limbs. In motion he appeared to be always staggering forward. There was little extra fat on his frame.

The boy and the old man walked back to the truck around the grove of trees. Strayhorn never took his eyes off the birds. As the sun began to warm the air, the starlings became more animated and alive. The squawking from the trees increased as groups of twos and threes flew away from the roost, moving out over the fields; the noise surged in intensity, changing from a roaring murmur to an angry buzz to a wail.

An hour later, Strayhorn and the boy were dressed for business. Randall wore a beekeeper's pith helmet with netting draped over the edge of the brim. The boy had on a baseball cap and ski goggles. Both wore a pair of leather work gloves.

"We were in the Sacramento Valley," Strayhorn said. "This would have been '67 or '68. California was a beautiful place back then, before the hippies fucked it up. That's where I met my first wife, Yolanda. Half Mexican, half Italian. You think dynamite is volatile?"

Strayhorn removed two cases of construction dynamite from the back of the truck along with fuses and two hundred feet of wire. He talked the whole time.

"We lived in a big Air Stream that looked like a giant beer can," Strayhorn said, picking up one of the cases. "One night I'm out with my buddies and you know how that goes. I get home a little late and she's sitting there calm as you please. 'Where you been?' she says. Drunk as I am, I say something clever like, 'none of your damn business.' She just smiles at me. I go into the bedroom and I'm asleep before I hit the mattress. She takes the top sheet and stitches it to the bottom sheet all the way around with me in the middle. Took her all night. There I am sewed into my own bed like some kinda human tortilla. Then she grabs a broom and begins to beat me senseless with the wooden end. I couldn't go nowheres. I rolled off the bed kicking and screaming. She never raised her voice, telling me that when she asks a civil question, she expects a civil answer."

The old man carried the explosives to the fence and carefully placed the dynamite on the ground.

"We was divorced a year later," he said. "Never marry a woman you're afraid to go to bed with."

Strayhorn pulled the wire apart and the boy wedged through. The boy and the old man moved through the field and into the trees carrying the dynamite and the rolls of wire. The air was cooler beneath the canopy. Strayhorn set the supplies down and scanned the upper branches.

"We're looking at close to a million starlings," he said, "and somewhere in here is the brains. Could be as few as half a dozen birds. Just like every animal on the planet there's leaders and followers. Starlings are no different."

Birds hopped from branch to branch, squabbling for room among the dark crowds. The squawking seemed to rise and fall in waves and in the lull the boy could hear individual birds mimicking human voices. 'Hello stranger,' one bird said. 'Praise Jesus,' said another bird, 'praise his name.' The screeching became louder, rolling down from the upper branches like a wave. They could feel the hissing and screaming pass over and through their bodies. And then, it was quiet. More quiet than it had been all morning. Strayhorn and the boy could hear the dry leaves under their boots.

"Let's get back to the truck, pronto," Strayhorn said. His voice sounded too loud in the unnatural silence. Strayhorn and the boy took a few steps and then the ground seemed to lift under their feet with a sulphurous rush of air and leaves and dust as the birds lifted from the trees as one body. They flew out from the roost in rings moving away from the center, growing wider and more sparse as the body grew distant from the brain. A dense, feathered surge of birds passed over Strayhorn and the boy as they ran toward the shelter of the truck, the sound like the deep hissing of the ocean as waves bite down on the sand. The mass of birds collided and wrestled for position within the moving flock: a city of birds falling horizontally through the air.

The two figures ran across the field and slid through the wire, the birdshit falling as dense as rain. Thick rings of starlings circled the trees in wide loops, moving out over the fields as more and more birds left the roost. Then the rings collided into clouds of birds and the clouds rolled through the air like dust before a storm. A hungry, black cloud with a million wings, the starlings dipped and dove and soared through the warm air, devouring grasshoppers and June bugs and mosquitoes in an aerial banquet at once sport and supper.

The flock was moving slowly across the dome of sky above the field. Smaller clusters of birds broke from the group and flew up and away from the mass, then turned back to re-join the group. The birds circled the field, gathering stragglers into the larger flock. The shriek from a million beaks found the same pitch. The boy dropped to the ground and pulled his hood over his head. The birds screamed at the base of his skull. Strayhorn stood beside him watching the starlings circle the field. The old man kept his eyes on the birds as they spun wildly over the ground like smoke rising from a fire. Then the flock turned to the south and flew away.

Strayhorn drove with his head out the window, searching the sky for the lost flock. The truck bounced down a dirt road, past fields of wheat and alfalfa, and rolled to a stop at county blacktop. In the distance the birds floated over the green fields like a dark fog. Strayhorn put his foot to the gas and the truck shot forward.

"These birds will move great distances to feed," Strayhorn said. "They may fly clear to the next county before landing."

"I didn't get any breakfast," the boy said.

"I can't stop now, boy. We're in the middle of an aerial pursuit."

The boy began to look around inside the truck for something to eat.

"See if you can find a map," Strayhorn said.

"Why don't we leave them alone?" the boy asked. "They're just birds. They're not hurting anybody."

Strayhorn's truck passed a farm convoy going the other way, a truck pulling a flatbed trailer, a combine, and a girl about the boy's age on an ATV. Strayhorn swerved into the grass at the side of the road, made a u-turn, and began to follow the girl. He pulled his truck up alongside her and she slowed to a stop. A dog stood on the back of the ATV.

"Ask her if she's seen any birds," Strayhorn said to the boy.

"You ask her. I'm not your slave." The boy slumped against the door to avoid looking at the girl.

"Hello," Strayhorn said. "Have you seen a flock of birds this morning?"

The dog started barking at the old man and the boy.

"Shut up, stupid," the girl yelled.

She reached for a phone on her belt and mumbled something into it. One by one the farm equipment pulled off the road into the grass and came to a stop. Strayhorn jumped out of his truck and stood in the grass scanning the sky. His eyes were never still; the slightest movement caused his head to dart to the source of the interruption. The farmer walked over to Strayhorn and the two men shook hands. He looked like every farmer Strayhorn had ever seen. Thick, red fingers, skin the texture of sandpaper. When the farmer pushed his hat back on his head, it revealed a broad section of white skin. He looked at Strayhorn with a skeptical grin.

"You're the bird man, ain't you?" the farmer said. Strayhorn smelled cigarettes, coffee, and whiskey. The farmer dug into his front pocket for his smokes. "How do you intend to eradicate these pests?"

"If I told you," Strayhorn said, "you wouldn't need me." The farmer took his time lighting his cigarette. Strayhorn stood motionless, except for a hand that jiggled the coins in his pocket. "My guess is that the birds are looking for fields where the grain is heavy on the stalk."

"That would be the whole fucking state," the farmer said.

The farmer spread a map out over the hood of the truck and the two men studied the tiny red and blue lines, the county boundaries, and state roads. The engine of the truck ticked as it cooled. The girl and the boy stood a few feet from each other watching the men, partners now against the adults and their map. She pointed toward the combine and they walked away unnoticed.

The boy sat in the driver's seat of the combine and looked down at the road and the fields, the wide blades of the machine spread out in front of him. He felt like he was inside a large, metallic beetle. The girl stood behind him. Her smell and heat filled the cab.

"I got a tattoo," she said. "Wanna see it?"

The boy was afraid to answer, afraid he might say the wrong thing and she would leave the cab and take her smell with her. He nodded his head. She turned her back and in one motion unzipped her jeans and pulled them over her hips. The boy was staring at the base of her spine and the words, "Having fun?" He could hear his own breathing become ragged and deep and he reached out to touch the words on her skin.

"Look," she said.

On the other side of the bug-smeared windshield, a long dark fog moved over the field like seeds floating over the ground. The girl quickly pulled up her jeans, opened the cab door, and shouted.

"We found 'em!"

Strayhorn and the farmer looked up from the map.

The farmer drove the lumbering combine with the girl sitting next to him. With the walkie-talkie close to her mouth, she kept up a running commentary on the flight of the birds. Strayhorn and the boy followed in their truck with a walkie-talkie of their own. Between her words the boy listened to her breathing coming through the air and out of the metal box in his hand.

The flock moved across the landscape, a dark liquid poured on a table. Thick channels of birds flowed over the fields, changing course, splitting, re-grouping, a dark, formless thing rolling through the blue air. The boy had seen this many times, and every time he had the same thought: Why do we have to kill them?

The boy looked at the farmer and his equipment and shook his head.

"I'm not sure what they see in this life," Strayhorn said. "Farmers, I mean. Long hours, short pay. Always behind on the work. Extremities of weather, isolation. Look at this place. Who in their right mind would settle out here? It's a life for a hermit or the worse kind of religious fanatic. The uncertainty of the elements has twisted their religious views. Their God is a distant, unhappy deity who expresses his love through drought and storm. His benevolence is measured by the amount of moisture in the soil at any given season. These people don't trust the government or cities or anyone who lives more than ten miles from their front door. You and me, boy, are just part of that ungrateful, ignorant mass of deadbeats, homosexuals, and bureaucrats who conspire to cheat these honest citizens at every turn. In their opinion, farming is the only noble occupation left to a man in this country, and yet every one of these boneheads is working off a mortgage handed to him by his father, who in turn had it handed to him by his father. A black hole of debt so deep they can't see the sky on a clear day. Out of the last thirty years I bet they've had two good growing seasons. And a good year is when they break even. That's a fucked-up business model."

"The birds have stopped," the girl said. "No, wait. They're circling. Now they're moving again."

The vehicles rolled through an open wire gate and into a wide field of wheat. The combine stopped and the truck rolled up behind it. Bird stragglers joined the mass and swirl. The flock twisted and dove as the bird cloud gained height and rose above the field like a thunderhead. With each turn over the wheat, the starlings gathered closer together, like water churning toward a drain. The sound was unearthly: a long scream, a roar, a vibration that disrupted thought. And then, as though a drain had been opened, the birds funneled down, dropping rapidly, and fell hard on the grain.

The boy grabbed his father by the sleeve and pointed out into the field. A man stood hip deep in the wheat, firing a shotgun at the birds falling around his head. The gun's muzzle flashed with fire, but the only sound was the screaming birds. Strayhorn plunged into the field. The man lowered the gun and shouted something. Strayhorn grabbed the man's arm and pulled him toward the truck.

The birds had landed. Birds on top of birds. The first wave fighting for position, flapping and jumping. The stalks of wheat bent over and in seconds were stripped of grain. And then the next wave of starlings and the next, as the descending weight of the birdcloud crushed the field. The beaks of a million starlings snapping and slashing at the grain like the cutlery of angry diners.

Strayhorn and the boy worked through the night. The light from the kerosene lanterns threw their exaggerated shadows up into the canopies of the trees; Strayhorn, the larger figure, carried the dynamite, and the boy, his giant offspring, carried the wire. The boy spooled out the wire up the rough trunks and out to the extremities of the branches, hopping from limb to limb.

In the morning the trees were still empty except for a few lonely, squawking sentry birds. The boy set up a tent on a hill a few hundred yards from the trees, crawled inside, and fell asleep. Strayhorn slept in the truck.

The boy woke up in the early evening and heated a can of soup over a camp stove. Strayhorn stood with his hand over his eyes and scanned the horizon.

"Do you want some soup?" The boy shouted, knowing his father would refuse. His old man had strange ideas about food and disease. His favorite breakfast was a fried egg sandwich with the bread soaked in the grease of the pan. He'd drown the sandwich in ketchup and salt and pepper, then eat it standing up. Another of his theories: a sitting position encumbered digestion.

Father and son sat on the grass and watched the sun go down and the night come up. The stars blinked down on them and Strayhorn began to name the constellations and talk about the stars and the different levels of brightness and what that meant.

"Just shut up," the boy said. "Can't we just sit and look at something without having to name it or know every god damn thing about it."

The boy stood up and walked away from the fire to pee and then went into his tent. Strayhorn stretched out on the grass and fell asleep. When he opened his eyes, it was morning. A few of the brightest stars were still visible like silver coins at the bottom of a pool.

The clouds that day swept across the sky in thin trails, white, see-through curtains drifting and re-forming as the heated currents carried the moisture aloft. Strayhorn walked across the field and into the trees carrying a rifle. He could hear the rustling and movement of wings in the branches. A few birds called to each another. The old man spotted a single starling on an upper limb. He could see the bird's yellow eyes. Strayhorn lifted the rifle and fired. The bird jumped from the branch and fell to the ground. It lay on its back, wings pulling at the air, its beak opening and closing. Strayhorn nudged the bird with the barrel of the rifle.

"You don't belong here. Why are you here?"

All afternoon the sky was an empty blue arena; until just before sundown, clouds moved across the roof of air. The blue sky suddenly turned red from the dust of a storm created days earlier, somewhere out west. The red dust particles created spokes of crimson that illuminated the sharp edge of the horizon, and as the sun descended it dropped behind the treeline, erasing the light along its retreating path. With each revolution, the world was brought closer to zero.

Strayhorn and the boy made sandwiches with white bread, bologna, and mayonnaise and sat on the tailgate of the truck listening to the crickets in the fields. Strayhorn told the boy that when he was younger a grassland like this would light up with fireflies at dusk, a glowing universe hovering above the ground. But pesticides had killed them all. There weren't even any mosquitoes or moths or gnats now. Just the crickets.

"If the birds don't come back tonight," Strayhorn said, "we gotta go."

The boy worked his gum slowly like he was about to open his mouth and say something, but he didn't. Strayhorn unrolled his sleeping bag in the bed of the truck that night. For the first time in a long time he wanted a drink, but he'd given up alcohol years ago. He'd also given up reading. He loved books but it required a calmness and focus he could not sustain. He preferred to have someone read aloud to him. Perched on a chair, locked in on the rhythm of the voice, it was the only time he was ever still. Strayhorn had been married three times and each time had fallen for the woman because of the quality of her voice.

His second wife had been an alcoholic, a binge drinker. She could go months without a drink and then something would happen: a full moon, a bad memory, or just a few empty hours in the middle of the day that felt like an eternity. It was never the same thing twice, so there was no preparing for it. She would be gone for days. He'd get a call to come pick her up from a bar two towns over or the sheriff's office. The last time it happened she'd run off with a Marine just discharged from the service. After a few drinks they'd fallen in love. She was pretty quiet on the ride home, sitting in the front seat, staring out the window to avoid looking at her husband.

"It's a disease, Randall," she'd said finally.

"I had pneumonia last winter," he said. "You don't see me fucking the lady down the street."

The starlings came back that night all at once, re-invading the trees in clouds. They settled into the branches, folding their wings, walking the limbs until each bird found its perch in the roost—a shadow merging with its substance.

Strayhorn opened his eyes in the middle of the night and heard what he thought was the wind. He climbed out of the truck and walked down the hill toward the trees. He could feel the air vibrating; he could smell the salt, the sound of wings disturbing the air. The old man felt like the night had opened its mouth and had exhaled a river of birds.

The detonation box, dense and heavy as a car battery, was an ancient wooden contraption he'd bought in a junkyard in Nebraska. Strayhorn carried it out to the field a good two hundred yards from the trees, unspooling the wire, walking backward over the turned ground. The boy refused to help with this part of the operation. He stood in the grass with his hood cinched tight over his face.

The explosion started under their feet like a deep cough; the ground bulged up abruptly then fell back to its original position. The air rushed past them, away from the eruption, and then just as quickly rushed back toward the vacant center of the blast with the smell of birds and vegetation and torn limbs and shredded leaves and burnt feathers. The return of the air brought screaming and shrieking. Frantic wings slapping at the smoke, the dust, the fire. A fireball rolled in on itself and pulled everything into the center and up into the air, an expanding sphere of fire and dirt and green matter. The blast grew into the shape of a tree and blossomed up from the ground like new growth. The fire-tree built into a cloud that rolled and grew and moved higher into the blue sky until it lost momentum and the things it carried began to fall back to earth. Shattered tree branches and leaves and soil and wings and heads and feathers. Clumps of sod and chunks of burnt starlings and new things forged of separate entities in the blast. The boy saw a bird flying with a stick through its neck and another bird on the ground with one wing trying to right itself and fly. The dirt and gravel came down in a shower as though the explosion had created a new kind of weather. The feathers and bird parts and leaves and smoke drifted across the field. The explosion was over but the boy could still hear the eruption, could still feel the movement of hot air across his face, the smell of the charred birds now deep in his throat. Strayhorn stood looking at the place where the trees had once been, adjusting his vision to the new landscape. He held the rifle under his arm. His pockets were full of shells.

They waited until the smoke drifted past, then walked down the hill. The black framework of the grove was still burning and smoking. The skeletons of the larger trees remained upright, but the leaves and branches had been stripped from the trunks. The blast had knocked the birds out of the trees. Thousands moved aimlessly over the smoking ground. There was no squawking or calling, just the rustle of feathers as birds jumped and opened their wings, trying to lift themselves off the ground. But the explosion had damaged something; their wings didn't work right and they fell awkwardly. Others were missing vital parts: wings, beaks, feet, and still they twisted and maneuvered, frantic to separate from the earth. The boy tried to step around the dead and dying birds, but there were too many. A black choppy sea of starlings flowed around his feet.

Not from Around Here

A Conversation with Joe Totten

The following conversation was conducted by managing fiction editor James McNulty.

James McNulty: Hey, Joe! Congrats on landing the runner-up prize in our first Adrift Short Story Contest! We're excited to publish this brutal yet beautiful story about Strayhorn and his adversaries. Let's start with an easy question. Could you tell us a bit about how you came by the initial inspiration for this story?

Joe Totten: I was reading an article about the European Starling and how they came to be in North America. The starling was introduced by a man in NY. The bird is a non-native species with no natural enemies.

Over the years the starling population increased so dramatically that they became a threat to crops. The article referenced a program in California in the 1970s that killed several million starlings. I began to imagine what kind of person would choose to go from farm to farm, killing birds, and I came up with Randall Strayhorn.

JM: Was the program mentioned similar to how Strayhorn dealt with the starlings? That is to say, how much of his process is fictionalized, and how much is researched?

JT: They sprayed a toxic substance on the birds, not sure what it was. But I wanted something a little more flashy, so I added the dynamite.

JM: Is this often how ideas for new stories come to you—through reading other media?

JT: Sometimes. My day job is copywriter for an ad agency, and most of my reading at work is around technology. My reading habits away from work are very eclectic.

I just published a book, *The Law of Capture*. It's a novel about the American West, and for that book I read a lot of history, memoirs, and firsthand accounts of the west.

I'm writing a crime novel now, set in the 1970s. So I'm reading a lot of newspaper archives and books about that era. My ideas for stories don't seem to follow any particular pattern.

JM: Congratulations on your book publication! Hearing that you work in advertising meshes well with the idea that you added dynamite to the story to make it "more flashy." Could you talk a little about how working in advertising has influenced your writing?

JT: There are both good and bad influences associated with working at an agency. Ad work demands that you write every day; sometimes it's only a few paragraphs, but those paragraphs have to tell the whole story. There's a demand that the writer get to the point quickly. There' s little room for extraneous description. As a result, I think my writing is very spare, stripped down to the essential narrative. I've been fortunate to practice my craft every day for more than twenty years, so I've learned discipline and to work to deadlines. On the negative side, grammar and punctuation are not as critical, as you well know after reading my story.

JM: That sounds like a great recipe for tight writing. Don't be too self-deprecating; there wasn't so much cleaning needed for the grammar and punctuation as you suggest. It always surprises me, but I've met other copywriters who admit to the same fault. Is grammar and punctuation not so important when writing for advertisements? On a more micro-level, how do you think writing ads for so long has shaped your approach to language when writing fiction—regards sentence structures, interesting uses of punctuation, and innovative phrasing? There are so many beautiful sentences in this story—particularly those describing birds and their movements.

JT: Advertising is all about new/different/unique. As a writer I would churn through dozens of phrases looking for that special one that would say what I wanted to say without sounding trite or corny. I have always tried to avoid cliché. Advertising writing is constantly constrained by the medium. Thirty seconds is thirty seconds. You have to write to the space you are given. You are always trying to say more with less, and often traditional punctuation and sentence structure has to be modified or abandoned altogether.

JM: So advertising forces creativity through the limitations it imposes; the same argument is often made in favor of prompts and forms of poetry, but you don't often hear it in terms of advertising. There's a clear love of language—love of "new/different/unique"—on display here. There are so may gorgeous descriptions of birds in this story. Do you do a lot of bird-watching? We've already determined that you'd prefer to fictionalize than to research—at least in terms of adding dynamite. Is it the same case for your descriptions? Asked another way: how do you mine the description of the flocks of birds—through abstract thought alone or through watching them in real life or in videos?

JT: I live in a small town in northern Utah, surrounded by mountains. We are also surrounded by wildlife. I do a lot of casual bird-watching, I don't keep a list or anything, but listening to and watching birds is a lifelong habit. Birds have always fascinated me.

JM: Quick question from our editor Dan Leach: "One of the first things that strikes a reader is how sensual and lyrical the language is. In fact, the several pages contain little dialogue and almost no interiority, instead doing the wonderful trick of leveraging sensory impressions and landscape to reveal character. Talk to us about the challenges and advantages of working in this style. Is it a style you've always worked in or one that developed over time?"

JT: Hmm. That's a tough one to answer. I don't believe I have a discernible style. I'm writing a crime novel right now that is almost all dialogue. I do have a bias toward action in stories and novels. "The Starling Killers" is story that came from a central action: two men trying to kill a large flock of starlings. Landscape is important, the movement of the characters over that landscape is critical. The movement of the birds through the landscape is also important. The story takes place outside, so description of land and sky became essential to the narrative. I am fortunate to live in a place where I notice the changes in the environment as the weather and the seasons move through. I suppose if I lived in Brooklyn, I'd be writing a different type of story.

JM: The writing shifts to meet the story's demands on its own terms; makes sense to me. I want to shift topics a bit here to ask about the role politics play in a story. Often, the stories we receive are too overt in their political messaging or risk preaching to the choir. Strayhorn makes a point of talking about the farmer's politics, but the story never bashes us over the head with any political messages. Strayhorn does, though, seem a very emblematic character. What does he represent to you?

JT: Is Strayhorn emblematic of a certain political or cultural view? I tried to create a three-dimensional character with the old guy. He's a mashup of several people I have known over the years, but he's an individual. Everyone is entitled to his or her interpretation of this story, but I push back a little on placing any of these characters in a category. It spoils the fun. I guess it's understandable given the times we live in.

JM: If your protagonist were a paper-thin character who only served as a stand-in for an idea, we wouldn't be publishing your story. That said, I do think it's possible for a complex, multi-faceted character to also represent something larger. A character may be an individual, but the themes that the character deals with are also what they're emblematic of. Let's tackle this question a different way. What role, if any, do you think politics serves in this story? Particularly Strayhorn's monologue about the farmers and how they feel about Strayhorn and his son.

JT: When I started this story several years ago, this country was in the middle of a debate about who is and who is not allowed into the country. Native, non-native, immigrants, refugees. And we are still talking about it. Strayhorn's rant about the farmers was about highlighting one particular xenophobic point of view. If you're not from around here, then you must be suspect. And yet Strayhorn himself is guilty of that kind of thinking when he says that the starlings are not native to this country and don't belong here. It was my way of showing that if you take a broad enough view, no one, excluding Native Americans, are native to the ground they stand on. We're all unwelcome visitors.

JM: Another question from Dan Leach: "*Driftwood* has published numerous pieces that feature stories-within-stories, such as Strayhorn's marriage memories. Why deliver these via monologue as opposed to memory? The monologues work well in this story; do monologues frequent your other works, or was it Strayhorn specifically who demanded to speak?"

JT: Strayhorn just seemed like the kind of guy who would rant about certain subjects. He might even talk out loud to himself. Plus, I wanted the contrast between a father and son, where the father talks too much and the son rarely speaks. I looked at a few of my stories and there were some extended monologues, so I guess that's a feature of my writing I hadn't noticed.

JM: There's quite a lot of entertainment in those monologues. The joke about Strayhorn having pneumonia, though perhaps crude, still gets me every time I read it. It sounds like monologues come somewhat naturally to you—and you're good at writing them. What was the hardest part of writing "The Starling Killers"?

JT: This was a fairly easy story to write. I had to do some research about the origin of the starling in N. America—not hard, just time consuming. I guess the most difficult part was making Strayhorn sound believable.

JM: Which part of "The Starling Killers" was conceived of first? Was there anything in your original conception of the story that did not make it in?

JT: I started with a single idea. Starlings were massacred in large flocks in the 1970s. I went from that idea to a crazy man and his son traveling the country killing birds. In an early draft of the story, Strayhorn created a huge metal tree, and when the starlings landed on the branches, he flipped a switch and electrocuted the birds. But then I thought dynamite is easier and more portable.

JM: That sounds fun, albeit a bit cartoonish; the dynamite seems to promise more gorgeous imagery, though. It's been said that every story has one moment (or line) that is so vital to the heart of the story that if it were removed the whole story would—pardon the pun—implode. What, in this story, is that moment? Do you have a favorite line from this story?

JT: My favorite line is: "The beaks of a million starlings snapping and slashing at the grain like the cutlery of angry diners." I think the heart of the story is the explosion and without it the story would just be a crazy old man and his weird son. The explosion pulls the two factions of the story together.

JM: Do any other mediums/artforms influence you and your work?

JT: I would say the biggest influences on my work besides books are movies and music. I'm envious of musicians and directors who, with a few notes or images, can create a fully realized story. While it takes writers pages to build that kind of narrative.

JM: Which musicians and directors in particular?

JT: I like just about everything that Stanley Kubrick has done. Spike Lee and Kathryn Bigelow are two favorites; they've made some great films. Music is always changing and my tastes seem to change with it. But my favorites are: Miles Davis, Steely Dan, Etta James, Nina Simone, Aretha Franklin, and Amy Winehouse.

JM: Who are some of your favorite authors? Which authors influenced "The Starling Killers"?

JT: The writers I go back to over and over, either looking for inspiration or just to be entertained by their skill with words: Charles Portis, Cormac McCarthy, Elmore Leonard, Jorge Luis Borges, and Walter Benjamin.

JM: All *Driftwood* fiction goes through several rounds of comprehensive line-edits. We believe in polishing our fiction to its utmost potential. Could you talk a bit about the process of working through revisions with *Driftwood Press*? What do you make of the process of working through your work with an editor?

JT: I'm still learning the publishing business, so initially the editor's comments and suggestions weren't well received by me. But once I understood that the intent was to create a better story, I began to see the light. Going forward with my other work, I realize that a good, intelligent editor is essential to the process.

JM: I'm glad that your opinion of the usefulness of editors has been changed through working with Felicia and I. You mentioned a novel earlier. Where can readers pick up your novel? Have you published any other short stories or poems elsewhere?

JT: My new novel *The Law of Capture* is available on Amazon. I just released it a few weeks ago. I published two short stories a few years ago in a non-defunct magazine called the Wasatch Journal.

JM: Before we wrap up, is there anything else you'd like to tell us about this work in particular?

JT: No, I think we covered everything. I'm excited to see the story in print. Thanks for all your help and encouragement.

"CROW & KEY" | ALEXANDER LANDERMAN

I WAS A TEENAGE QUADRUPED

ZACHARY WILLIAMS

When I met you they'd cut seams
out of your jeans, sewed them into skirts
with the lance

of Longinus. "Not our thing, but it'll make her more
biblical," they said. I was hiding in the air conditioning
duct in the Kingdom Hall. No one was

smiling, especially the women. They'd spent
all day building a moat around the place
while men watched, sipping Tab.

Next Chinese New Year: reclined
on a rock in the middle of a river, no ants bit us.
You stood before the largest stone I've ever seen.
I swam to join you, unable able to scale it.
We stood for a long time in its shadow. Dazzled.
A Golden Retriever hopped right to the top,

and the thought of you small made me
so angry I transformed into a goat,
followed you knock-kneed to the bank.

You tried feeding: a pear, grapefruit
rinds, five nickel-sized stones.
I took only to a bottle filled with Tab.

When the antlers came, you used them
as candelabras, always finding ways
to make me dazzle.

But I grew heavy, obstructed
entry to restaurants and truck stop
commodes, got us kicked out everywhere.

You read in the Yee Naaldlooshii Encyclopedia
about a shamaness who could make me
boyish again. Loaded into your back seat,
I made it halfway through Wyoming

before finding my own kind queued
outside a rest stop refuge, their quadrilateral eyes
glowing under street lamps. I butted the wind-

shield until it shattered, arched through, smoke
of munitions factories in the middle distance.

I woke up making toast,
but used too-small bread.
It sank to the bottom, burned
on only one side. Not thinking

I jammed a fork in to claw it out,
got zapped, so good and zapped
my mind went white.

Through the spots in my eyes I spied
the postman through the window,
crowned by tree limbs.

Your letter open on the table, the date
indicating four years in wilderness,

and that goes for both of us. Both
moving toward a time and place
where all versions of ourselves collapse
into something workable:

restoration of my tongue, opposable
thumbs. Return of your eyes and arms,
your stolen wonder. I'm so glad

you're thriving, finding the faces
in the faux-wood paneling on your walls less frightening.

It's the definition of good to know
the asteroid landed just adjacent to your house.

INTERVIEW

ZACHARY WILLIAMS

First, let me say we could not be more in love with "I Was a Teenage Quadruped" and are honored to have it in our issue! I want to start off by diving right into the poem's opening and it's cryptic ceremony of converting jeans into skirts. Why did you choose to open the poem with this haunting, ritualistic scene? What role, if any, does religion play?

The religious aspects of the poem, for me, are there to lend the otherwise nonsensical situations a framework. There's an irony here, but also, I think, an element of truth in presenting these absurd, somewhat ominous rituals. The construction of a moat and the sewing of jeans into skirts suggest fundamentalism and isolationism of a kind, which the speaker helps the "you" break out of. Still, the speaker is perhaps not trustworthy as a guide away from this kind of fundamentalism. We're all guilty of stridency, especially when it comes to things we don't understand. Youth finds us at our most open, but it also makes us impatient and stubborn, though we like to think that's not the case.

Midway through the poem, the speaker transforms into a goat. However, the "you" of the poem never transforms or turns animalistic. What is the significance of this one-sided alteration?

For me, the animal transformation functions as an invitation for the masculine speaker—the speaker is masculine—to eschew his own responsibility toward self-actualization or address his own rage and responsibility in the disintegration of the relationship. It's worth noting that the resumption of his human form comes purely by accident. The "you," on the other hand, has to work, not only for themselves, but for him. It's unfair, and I think the tension of the poem resides in whether or not the speaker is aware of these facts during his recollection. I like to think he is, but readers may think otherwise, which is a good thing.

The majority of the poem is comprised of three-line stanzas, with slightly longer ones interjecting throughout. Was this the structure of the poem from the beginning, or did it change?

Strangely enough, this poem first started taking shape in 2011 as a prose poem. From there, I began expanding on the content and breaking it up into stanzas. The process was purely intuitive. The structure revealed itself through the accumulation of images, what I felt was the natural momentum of the poem's narrative. I try not to get too stuffy about structure. The key concern is that the content of the poem feels delivered in a way that feels necessary, that each line and stanza carries the weight it needs to.

As an editor few things excite me more than a strong last line, and yours is truly exceptional. I love the concluding sense of relief in being adjacent to danger, in being nearly destroyed. How did this final, stark line come to you? Was the idea of ending with an image of near-devastation intentional?

To say the ending image was intentional may be a stretch, but upon reflection I think it serves as an acknowledgment of the gravity of the "you"'s situation in contrast with the speaker's. Still, a number of other explanations and associations come to mind. I think a lot of it has to do with distinguishing between what things we can choose to act upon and what things tumble down upon us. It also lets the "you" be lucky for the first time in the poem, which feels an appropriate way to end things after all that's happened.

How much revision went into this poem?

I've been working on this poem, in multiple forms, since 2011. It began as a prose poem, but as I continued working on it, it became obvious that blocks of text weren't going to lend it the structure or pacing it needed. The situation that inspired it also changed, so adjustments were made in that regard. I don't usually take seven years to complete a poem, but sometimes certain ones stick in the mind and convince you that they're never finished. I'm glad that I've given myself enough time to grow with this one.

Is this poem categorical of your work? Why or why not?

I would say so. I'm always trying to find some way of transacting boredom, anxiety, and the like into something more imaginative, more constructive. I wouldn't say my poetry is steadfastly political, but I do believe that the ethos behind it is. Imagination is key to transcending this strange, lonely period in which we all live. I want my work to give people something to look at, something that pushes against the regimented and unimaginative, past atomization and into a collective commiseration, if not celebration, of the fact that this condition is shared in some fashion.

If you had to narrow it down, what three books have had the most impact on your writing?

Paterson by William Carlos Williams cracked my head open in a way that was utterly necessary. I love books that destroy temporality in that fashion and, thus, approach timelessness. Virginia Woolf's *The Waves*. I love the shifting landscape and the near-monotone polyphony of it. David Berman's *Actual Air* is the first poetry collection I ever bought and read, and I read it at least once a year. That was 2008 or 2009. It's been with me a while and never stops growing on me.

Based on your personal experience, what advice would you give to other writers?

Always keep working. Don't wait; stay active in even the worst of circumstances. Some say you shouldn't approach anything in a bad mood, but I don't think that's particularly good advice. Perseverance is key. But also, perspective: it's good to keep in mind that no one has asked you to do this, and so nothing is owed for the effort except the enjoyment of amusing yourself. Eventually, you find that you amuse others.

Where can readers find more of your work?

I've got some work up at *Juked, FORTH Magazine,* and *Mush/Mum. Mush/Mum*'s staff gives particular attention to its presentation, so it's always a treat to see what they've managed to pull off on the design side of things.

What drew you to *Driftwood Press?*

I'm always attracted to smaller presses. They tend to take more risks. I also liked the visual design of many of the issues, as well as the work. I appreciate when magazines can publish poems with lovely horses, then you turn the page and there's slime everywhere. I like horses and I like slime and rarely ever get to see them together.

ALBERT LEE

1 Baba graduated from Japanese school in 高雄, Taiwan at 16. He completed his military service at 22. He came to Hawai'i with $4,000, a gun, and a box of his grandmother's 割包 at 25.

2 I graduated from high school in Honolulu, Hawai'i at 17. Next fall, I'm going to Tokyo with a credit card, a Moleskine, and a box of my great-grandmother's 割包. I will be 21.

3 In Hawai'i, Baba needs an ID to buy groceries because he's an alcoholic. Yikes.

4 In Minnesota, the white kids don't think I speak English and the Chinese kids don't think I speak Chinese. Surprise, 傻逼s.

5 Baba had his money stolen by a 老黑 on his first week in America and he's high-key hated black people ever since. He ended up working ninety hours a week as a dishwasher at an izakaya for two months. The dish room smelled like a white dude jogging in the middle of August.

6 I lost my grandmother's ox horn comb at a night market in 臺北. I told Baba someone stole it because I didn't want him to hit me. Baba then spent three weeks scouring the night market, trying to find the motherfucker I vaguely described to him. The hairs on his arms were like blackened grass waiting for the smell of a monsoon.

7 When I was 7, I told Baba my throat hurt. He told me it was because I forgot to take out the trash. I took out the trash and my throat still hurt. So Baba shoved *ryukakusan* herbal lozenges down my throat. My throat still hurts.

8 Am I Baba's Anglophone dream?

9 When Baba was 16, he told my grandmother he didn't want to go to Japanese school anymore because it was 1967 and Japan lost the war. My grandmother said she'd decapitate his girlfriend and hang her head over the kitchen stove. Whenever he speaks Japanese, his throat hurts.

10 Oh. Is Baba my Japonic fantasy?

11 Baba started shooting the Panasonic air conditioner because the low hum annoyed him. Afterward, he told me: 「孩子，你不是日本的小蹄子。」 Child, you are not Japan's bitch.

12 Cousin Rachel and I decided to study abroad in Japan as a means to make Japan our bitch, to understand our post-colonial positionality in relation to 大日本帝國, The Empire of Great Japan.

13 As of 1898, when China ceded Taiwan to Japan, Baba does not speak Japanese anymore.

十四 何語であっても、ババとどうやって話せばいいのか分かりません。

(**14** I don't know how to talk to Baba in any other language.)

INTERVIEW

ALBERT LEE

What inspired the poem?

Starting this September, I will be studying abroad at Waseda University in Tokyo, Japan. As a result, I've been thinking a lot about my positionality in relation to Japan as a Taiwanese American, as the diaspora of a postcolonial subject. For more than a hundred years now, whereas Amis & Hokkien have always been my family's mother tongues, Mandarin, Japanese, and more recently, English have been the languages through which we interact with people outside of the home. And so this piece was inspired by broader questions about linguistic imperialism, Japanese empire, and hyphenated identity. Essentially, what does it mean for your second or third language to be better than your first because of circumstances beyond your control?

Is there anything unique about your personal writing process?

I was born and raised in Honolulu, Hawai'i, where I was fortunate enough to be exposed to many different languages and literatures from a very young age. As a result, my writing spills between languages and cultures. If I had to quantify it, about 40% of my thinking happens in English, another 40% happens in Hokkien, Mandarin, or Cantonese, another 10% happens in Japanese, and the last 10% is done in French, Korean, or some other language that I've managed to pick up along the way. As such, when I write a poem in English, I amalgamate different linguistic fragments and choose which of these bits to translate into English and which to render in the original thought. As a result, there are at least four languages living in this poem.

How much revision went into this poem?

In terms of major revisions, not much, to be honest. I've been working on a sequence of prose sonnets for the past year and a half, and so I was quite comfortable writing through the poem. I made some changes here and there when deciding which words to leave in the original language and which words to italicize or translate, but I wrote the poem in half an hour and probably spent another half-hour doing edits for cohesiveness. As my advisor, Ping Wang, would say, "You've been metaphorically writing this poem your entire life and now you've finally sat down and physically regurgitated it onto a piece of paper."

What is your favorite line from the poem or the line you are most proud of?

My favorite line is definitely, "The hairs on his arms were like blackened grass waiting for the smell of a monsoon." It was a thought that originally came to me in Hokkien and after doing a quick translation of it into English, that's what I got.

Who are some of your favorite poets?

I currently work at a bookstore and so I've been fortunate enough to get an advanced copy of Ocean Vuong's forthcoming novel, *On Earth We're Briefly Gorgeous*, an intensely fragile masterpiece. In particular, it was really interesting to read it in conversation with his previous book of poetry, *Night Sky With Exit Wounds*. In both his novel and in his poetry, you can see Ocean use form as an extension of content, something that I often think about as I write my sequence of numbered, prose sonnets. Moreover, though Ocean Vuong is my current obsession, I also really love Layli Long Soldier, Justin Chin, Jericho Brown, Jos Charles, Bei Dao, Yang Lian, Tanikawa Shuntaro, Sugimoto Maiko, Kim Hyesoon, François Cheng, and Gao Xingjian.

If you had to narrow it down, what three books have had the most impact on your writing?

Oof. This is such a hard question. The book of all books, however, would definitely have to be Marcel Proust's *À la recherche du temps perdu* (*In Search of Lost Time*). I first came across excerpts of the book in AP French class, and since then, it's been a really good book for thinking about the links between memory and trauma. On a side note, if you can read Chinese, Zhou Kexi does a phenomenal translation of it, as well. With that said, the second book of all books would be Arthur Sze's miraculously mundane, *The Ginkgo Light*, and the third and final book would be **金瓶梅** (*The Golden Lotus*), a sexy, Chinese classic that is probably still banned in China because of its salacious content.

Do you work in any other mediums? How do those other genres inform your poetry?

I recently quilted a denim, patchwork quilt for a final project in one of my classes. I see quilting to be very similar to poetry in that you're given all of these interesting fragments and have to somehow find the thread which sews them together into one, coherently beautiful piece.

Based on your personal experience, what advice would you give to other writers?

Get on poetry Twitter. It's an infinitely amusing place where you can get to know the humans behind the poets you love and get up-to-date notifications on poetry submissions, contests, and other good poetry-related juju. Also, the memes. Omg, the memes. i lub te memes uwu.

8 Indian River Road

RAINIE OET

Diane and I on the slide in the river a black leech
clinging to my shoulder or hers the slide floating in the shallow
water near the shore Mama watched us one of us had to
hold the slide down so the other could slide down it we were that light
I yelped and pulled the leech away Mama spun around
like a puppet on untangling strings held by a cloud she lifted
her head from her newspaper we tried to look at her
she had no face a black cloth had been sewn onto it

Almost Drowning

Rainie Oet

Diane took me out from the shore. I went with her toward the floating station people were diving a quarter mile away.

Less than halfway there I said I can't make it.

Why are you stopping, she said—I feel like I could swim forever.

I think I would drown, I said—I don't even know if I can make it back.

It's an equal distance there or back, she said.

I want to go back, I said.

I think that is the last time she trusted me. Before she died I almost died. Now I wonder what would have happened if I kept going?

We could have kept going. I thought I was going to die.

I don't remember how long we swam back because it was infinite.

I hugged the sand and panted for ten unbroken minutes.

I REMEBER NOT SLEEPING

SHERRI LEVINE

I remember lying on a squeaky cot, in a room full of Czech women,
listening to them breathe like lung machines.

I remember steam hissing from radiators, heels clicking down halls.

I remember, on the psychiatric ward, thinking that the patients were doctors
who were there to save me because I was dying.

A flashlight shone in my eyes every two hours during the night,
a needle poked my arm.

Someone always watched me in the shower with a flashlight.

I remember waking up at night to use the bathroom
and seeing Czech nurses watching porn on TV.

I remember having sex with men, multiple men, and women,
but I don't remember feeling anything except sore.

I was never tired. And never hungry.

I got a day pass from the hospital and snuck into a man's car.
We smoked unfiltered Camels and listened to Metallica.

I hated heavy metal, but it felt good to be held.

I remember the doctor asking me if I had been breastfed,
and what it meant to throw stones in glass houses.

I was afraid if I didn't get the answers right, something bad would happen to me.
One doctor said sleep deprivation causes mania.

My roommate swallowed a crushed light bulb.

I remember the bitter taste of pills I hid under my tongue.

I remember how good it was to come home—to stretch my legs across my bed, wrap myself
in clean, cotton sheets and listen to the rain.

Snow fell my last night in Prague before I got on a plane to the States.

I wasn't sure I would come back, but I wasn't thinking about that. I'd have to be up for 20 hours or more
to get home.

Interview

Sherri Levine

What inspired the poem?

This poem, "I Remember Not Sleeping," was inspired by a terrifying experience I had while I stayed in a psychiatric hospital in Prague, Czech Republic.

What was the hardest part about writing it?

I wanted to write from a distant emotional state. I wanted it to have a wider contextual meaning, something that wasn't just about me and my experience.

Compared to American hospitals I had stayed in, I found it remarkable how the Czech nurses and doctors treated me as well as the other patients. Even though the nurses could only speak a little English, they treated me with dignity and respect. For example, in the Czech hospital, I could wear my own clothes, isolations rooms didn't exist, and the community of women patients supported and comforted each other in a way I had never seen before in U.S. psychiatric hospitals.

What came easiest when writing this poem?

After reading Joe Brainard's memoire, *I Remember*, I realized I had a framework of how to write my poem.

How much revision went into this poem?

There were so many images to write about that it was a challenge of how to choose the most poignant ones.

Is this poem categorical of your work? Why or why not?

Many of my poems are different from each other. I wrote a book of persona poems, called *In These Voices,* published last year. "I Remember Not Sleeping," however, is one of the most honest poems I have ever written, the one I have felt the most vulnerable reading in front of an audience.

What is your favorite line from the poem or the line you are most proud of?

"I remember how good it was to come home—to stretch my legs across my bed, wrap myself in clean, cotton sheets and listen to the rain."

I think we can all relate to coming home to our beds after being with unpleasant or unfamiliar people or places or both.

Who are some of your favorite poets?

Langston Hughes, Theodore Roethke, Gwendolyn Brooks, Frank O'Hara, Robert Lowell, Dorianne Laux, Ellen Bass, Tony Hoagland, Peter Sears, and Andrea Hollander.

Where can readers find more of your work?

Timberline Review, Hartskill Review, The Sun Magazine, Verseweavers," Postcards Poets and Poems, Willawaw Review, VoiceCatcher, A Journal of Women's Voices & Vision. My chapbook, *In These Voices*, is published by *The Poetry Box.*

COLD CASE FICTION

LAWRENCE LORRAINE MULLEN

i.
02/01/1959: dyatlov pass incident[1]

05/12/1963: radiation from ural mountains makes it uninhabitable

07/23/1970: new aerial photographs show a commune at the foot of kholat syakhl

11/10/1975: ss edmund fitzgerald sinks in the great lakes[2]

09/08/1977: mass hysteria in lakeside wisconsin town

03/17/1981: cdc on high alert in michigan

04/22/1984: five midwest states are under military quarantine

ii.
there was a fight between who would stay and who would swim through the atlantic
no one wanted the job of pulling a thousand ton ship from the bottom of a lake

they all agreed to swallow their x ray pills and play rock paper scissors
five sighed in annoyance and trudged off / making sure their eyes stayed still in their sockets

the remaining four set up a more substantial camp
they expected to be there for a while and wanted their friends to return to a warm beverage

navigating through freezing tributaries was harder than expected
and all of them grieved for the limbs they lost along the way

when they found the ship's anchor and bow and railings
they dragged and dragged and dragged the corroded ship to shore

one didn't want to return and decided to take up motherhood however she could
and the remaining four became unintentional immigrants because she had been their navigator

and they couldn't help their bodies beginning to thaw when the spring came
they couldn't tell their rotting flesh from the asphalt and gravel.

---

[1]The Dyatlov Pass Incident refers to the unsolved deaths of nine college-aged hikers in the Ural Mountains between February 1 and 2, 1959. During the night the group camped out, something caused them to tear their way out of their tents and flee—when their bodies were found, several had died of hypothermia, while others had massive traumatic head and torso injuries, and one final member was missing her tongue and eyes.

[2]The SS Edmund Fitzgerald was an American freighter that sank during a storm in Lake Superior on November 10, 1975—its entire crew was lost.

Interview

Lawrence Lorraine Mullen

What inspired the poem?

This poem was originally a Charles Bernstein exercise that after a few rounds of revisions turned into what it is now. The exercise involved using dates and events that were both real and imagined. I chose to use footnotes to explicitly show which events were true, mostly because the events I used have a sort of not-real quality in the nature of the event (such as the Dyatlov Pass Incident, which is just wild).

How long do you usually spend working on a single poem?

It really depends—I tend to revise while I write or immediately after, like if I'm doing a quick read through and realize a word doesn't look or sound right, or a line feels off, etc. Sometimes a poem will feel near finished just after that brief revision. I've also written poems that have taken me a year to finish because I just can't quite pick a word that sounds right, or I just can't get the last stanza to say what I want it to.

How long have you been writing poetry? What has changed from your first poem to your newest work?

I've been writing poetry since high school, I was in the poetry club. I honestly couldn't say what my first poem was about, but I did use poetry alot back then to process mental illness (or rather, I didn't know it was mental illness then, it was just a blur of feelings). I wouldn't say that I don't write about mental illness anymore, but after time (and therapy and medication) it isn't as large of a part of my life anymore. My newer work focuses a lot more on bodies now and queer identities (and gothic-adjacent themes).

Who are some of your favorite poets?

I'm of course always reading and learning about new poets, but of who I've read so far, my favorite poets are probably Chen Chen, J. Jennifer Espinoza, Kaveh Akbar, Raquel Salas Rivera, and Ryan Eckes.

If you had to narrow it down, what three books have had the most impact on your writing?

I would say, at this point, probably *When I Grow Up I Want to Be a List of Further Possibilities* by Chen Chen, *Jane: A Murder* by Maggie Nelson, and *Franklinstein* by Susan Landers.

How would you personally define poetry?

I think of poetry as the act of making—or I guess the verb "to make." Poetry doesn't really feel like a noun to me I suppose; it feels like it is movement. I know that's a broad definition, but content matters less to me then it did when I was younger, in terms of what constitutes something being "poetic."

Based on your personal experience, what advice would you give to other writers?

I would say, "Inspiration can be bullshit." It really can be. Taking the time to write as often as you can, even if you don't necessarily feel "inspired" to do so, really helps you keep creating—and you don't have to keep everything you write, of course, and you shouldn't feel pressured to! Sometimes poems just don't work out and that's fine.

Where can readers find more of your work?

I don't have too many poems out and about right now, but you can find some of my work at *Maudlin House, Ghost City Review, Crab Fat Magazine, Meow Meow Pow Pow,* and *Fearsome Critters*!

Even David Had a Sex Tape

Stephen Hundley

And me at thirteen,
            finding them with their cases off
stacked like black plastic thigh bones
            before an altar and
swallowed by the VCR, the picture clipping,
            rolling in and out of the frame while
a host of fallen angels and I
            shimmy our pants to the floor.
The school bus is still roaring outside,
            and I'm savoring
Bathsheba on the shag carpet, Shadrach,
            Meshach, and a man in navy workpants
behind the camera saying: Jump
            in the oven, son. The water's fine.
I'm praying: Lord, make me a devil
            so I can stand the flames she's licking.

All these sins
            that turn my knees to jelly,
the static washing my body
            when I slump against the set.
I give a rainbow promise,
            then flood the screen again.
Daring the Lamb
            like my tongue on a battery,
and this one starts grainy
            with some kissing,
pans to David looking over the rooftops
            when she comes with her hair blown out
smacking gum and saying
            she's never done this.
And me at thirteen thinking:
            I've seen this one before.

INTERVIEW

STEPHEN HUNDLEY

What inspired the poem?

I grew up in a strange and intense place, religiously speaking. In South Georgia, the assumption was that you were some flavor of Christian—or that you were and didn't know it. There were no atheists, just folks lost somewhere in Doubt. A lot of opportunities for engaging in the community were church related. Picnics and trips to beaches and museums. School clubs. Even sports teams often had a religious element—organized prayers on the field, in the locker room, over the school intercom—things like that. The Bible felt like required reading in a lot of ways. It was the lingua franca between coaches, teachers, neighbors, girls, the rich and less-rich and less-less-rich.

Pondering The Bible, giving it a lot of consideration, while at the same time developing an understanding of my sexuality was an interesting, if ubiquitous, experience. The overlap of religion and hormones led to a lot of guilt and hard self-examination, but the parables I would read—especially in the Old Testament—would also colorize my experiences. Make them fantastical. It's my hope that "Even David Had a Sex Tape" taps in to some of that: struggling through what your body is telling you while religion shouts over it. Hearing both narratives at the same time and being pulled between them.

What was the hardest part about writing it?

I'm a fiction writer by training. A lot of the piece's early drafts were just big blocks of texts. I shifted things around endlessly. Line breaks and line logic continue to mystify me. I knew what I wanted to say, what struggle I wanted to portray, what images were moving the poem forward for me. What obsessed me. The challenge was arranging the form in a way that complimented the weird, wonderful parts—the mixing of the religious and the profane and the bodily. It took many drafts to pare the extra language away.

What came easiest when writing this poem?

Drawing on biblical allusions felt, at once, delicious and depraved. Revisiting those stories and looking, as I did in my childhood, for connections to my own heart was a lot of fun.

Is this poem categorical of your work? Why or why not?

Largely, yes. A good deal of my work focuses on my upbringing and using the South as a sort of wonderland where supernatural elements—Christian and otherwise—are ever-present and situated next to and over the mythology of the land, the old houses, the plants and animals. I don't often tackle the repercussions of church-culture on a character's mind, but I'm always interested in development. That is, how people feel out the line between right and wrong, belonging and exile, in the context of a place that they both love and fear.

What is your favorite line from the poem or the line you are most proud of?

"Jump / in the oven, son. The water's fine."

I've always been fascinated by trials of faith. Ordeals. For me, a lot of childhood and young manhood had to do with trials by fire, real or perceived. The story of Shadrach, Meshach, and Abednego has always interested me (if you're not familiar, it involves these guys getting thrown into a furnace), and to find the places that touched on faith, indulgence, guilt, and release was powerful and exciting—the places where that old world felt mapped over my living-world. I hope that comes through.

Is there anything unique about your personal writing process?

As I've said, prose is my first language. I start all of my poems with a free-write document where I just spew out ideas in paragraph form. From there, I break things into lines, rework ideas, trim and grow images. Sometimes I start over and write another paragraph. Slowly, something that looks like a poem emerges. Most of my poet friends go line-by-line with their pieces. For me, that invites too many opportunities for self-editing and doubt.

Who are some of your favorite poets?

I'm still cobbling together a pantheon of poets, reading everything I can find. I love reading literary magazines like *32 Poems, Carve, The Greensboro Review,* and *The Carolina Quarterly.* Of course *Poetry* and *Driftwood Press* (I bought Charles Malone's *Questions About Circulation* at AWP and loved it). I'll be honest and say that sometimes I'll latch on to a particular author and try to find more of their work, but generally I just let myself immerse in the work that's being produced and published right now. It's exciting—makes me feel like I'm communicating with a live community.

That said, I've been studying a lot of Frank Stanford's work—he's so weird and wonderful—and I was floored by Michael Bible's book *Sophia* (*Melville House* 2015). I was probably in my third re-read of *Sophia* when I wrote "Even David Had a Sex Tape."

How would you personally define poetry?

As I see it, the gift of poetry is obsession. While a lot of my verse is narrative, I really try to isolate and indulge ideas, to stay with them as long as possible and image-mine. The longer I think about something, the weirder the ideas surrounding it become, the brighter the colors in the language become. When I write prose I'm always juggling reader experience, character voice, and narrative arc—putting balls into the air and seeing them caught at the right moment later on. Writing poetry allows me time to sit with one feeling, one sentiment, one moment. I take a lot of pleasure in feeling out the boundaries, how deep that moment goes and what it rubs against.

GALE FORCE

AMY TROTTER

Dissecting an owl pellet,
we find a field mouse's
femur, skull, and jaw.

We find a crow's pelvis,
and you ask about death
on our short walk home.

I let your little hands
palpate my belly, ask
where sister has gone.

I make up a story
of a wind named Morta
who flees from her cave,

over the mountains,
swoops between trees,
how she blows over

the earth, scattering
ice into the wild
palmetto's black mane.

Sometimes, I say,
the horse can shake
it out, release the shards

to melt back into the earth.
I think you understand.
I think I might too.

And when we wander
back through the forest,
search for early daffodils

breaking through, I see
on the abandoned barn's
pitched and sagging roof,

a head turned backwards,
an eye unblinking, a silence
that even a twig cant break.

INTERVIEW

AMY TROTTER

What inspired the poem?

"Gale Force" was inspired by a story of a friend (who is more like a sister). She and her son found an owl pellet with tiny bones inside of it. Before her second son was born, she lost a child within one hour of birthing him. This poem was an attempt to grapple with that loss and how we carry those connections with us into the natural world.

What was the hardest part about writing it?

The revision process. Revising is always hardest for me. I particularly struggled with the creation/destruction myth.

This poem sat for about a month to cure before I could revise. I worked on it for about a week or two, changing content and form, before feeling like it was close enough to "complete" to show people in the real world.

What came easiest when writing this poem?

The images. They seemed to already exist in my mind. As she told me the simple story of finding the pellet, it seemed as though this poem already existed for her.

Was there anything in your original conception that did not make it in?

Yes. The myth part looked much different. The form also went through several iterations before landing in tercets.

Is this poem categorical of your work? Why or why not?

Yes—this poem speaks heavily to other poems I have in my current collection. Loss, motherhood, and nature have a funny way of co-existing, and those three things seem to spiral my works together in surprising ways.

What is your favorite line from the poem or the line you are most proud of?

"I think you understand. I think I might too." It feels like a pivotal and critical line around which the whole poem orbits.

Is there anything unique about your personal writing process?

Yes and no. I think most writers, and poets in particular, mine for memories and images that are moving enough to be something on the page. So I meditate into banks of memory for those moments. What might be different is my obsession with thesauruses, dictionaries, textbooks, and encyclopedias—I use them sort of similarly to bibliomancy.

How long do you usually spend working on a single poem?

It varies wildly. I have worked on poems for more than four years, and I have felt confident in a poem after one week. I think more often than not, though, my average is around two to three months.

How long have you been writing poetry? What has changed from your first poem to your newest work?

I've been writing poetry seriously (i.e, not in a tween journal) since about nine years ago. My first poems really sucked. My poems now suck a little bit less. There is always room for improvement, but I think I am trying less now to be "poetic," which ironically helps the suck meter wane.

Who are some of your favorite poets?

Kim Addonizio, Ellen Bass, Kaveh Akbar, Jenny Xiu, Aracelis Girmay, Lucie Brock-Broido, and more. Too many to name, really.

If you had to narrow it down, what three books have had the most impact on your writing?

Helen Cisxous' *Three Steps on the Ladder of Writing* and Kim Addonizio's *Ordinary Genius*. The third is not a book, but *Poetry*'s poem-a-day podcast inspires me daily.

Do you work in any other artistic mediums? If so, how do those other genres inform your poetry?

I am a photographer. I feel like this photographer's perspective has given me a sort of prosthetic eye into memories and moments, to help write in a way that gives others a glance into a moment and see it as I do.

Where can readers find more of your work?

Potomac Review, *American Journal of Poetry*, *Mazzo Cammin*, and now *Driftwood Press*!

What drew you to *Driftwood Press*?

The aesthetic completely matches my style, and I feel like my voice could sing with all of the other voices being published here. It just felt right. Thank you for the opportunity.

Come Here

SARAH ANDERSON

The cardinal
slams itself against
the front window

even when it rains.
You are nudging garlic
through beet greens

in a cast iron skillet
and I remember
a man in a shed,

his studio, the door
opening to sunlight.
I grew up without

television. He grew
up without sight.
For a living, he shapes

wood into spoons
and small bowls.
"Let parts of your world

talk to each other," he said
to me or to himself.
"I know where you are."

I thought I was perceptive
until I found that photograph
from fourteen years ago.

On the great porch
of that house by the water,
we tried to catch lanterns

as they blew, hitting
their paper roundness
against the ceiling.

Across from the province
is the mainland. Across
the lawn, I see a woman

from Iceland claiming
to have never seen a firefly.
This drive has become

everything I can't say
to you. In slow, half-moon
strokes,

I will wipe your face
with a warm cloth.
This is all I can promise.

What inspired the poem?

One rainy day, I sat in my house and observed a cardinal repetitively flying into a window. This image was the starting point of this poem and became the opening line.

What came easiest when writing this poem?

Making associative leaps felt organic to me when writing this poem.

Was there anything in your original conception that did not make it in?

In my original draft, the man in the shed says more to me. When revising the poem, I thought his statements would have more weight if they were more sparse.

How much revision went into this?

As I do most of my poems, I revised this poem several times. The most significant change I made was to its shape. It used to be made of longer-lined stanzas before it became small tercets in a line down the page.

What is your favorite line from the poem or the line you are most proud of?

My favorite line from the poem is:

"In slow, half-moon / strokes, / I will wipe your face / with a warm cloth."

How long have you been writing poetry? What has changed from your first poem to your newest work?

I have been writing poetry since my senior year of high school. I would say what has changed the most between my first poem and my most recent work is that I have more restraint; I understand that leaving things out can be as powerful as putting them in a poem.

Do you work in any other artistic mediums? If so, how do those other genres inform your poetry?

I take photographs all the time—primarily with my iPhone but also with a Nikon 1.

My mother is a photographer, so I grew up with the idea of capturing images as central to my life. I absolutely see photography and poetry as intertwined. My images inform my poems and vice versa. Sometimes I consider my photographic images poems when I'm not writing poems.

Based on your personal experience, what advice would you give to writers?

My advice to any writer is to make time for your writing. That seems like simple advice but the phrase "make time" is important since the time may not just present itself.

What drew you to *Driftwood Press*?

To be honest, your website drew me to you. I love the aesthetic of the site and that led me to the writing.

This is Your Life Now with Epilepsy

Kristin LaFollette

the room was cold and I could smell the dried blood from your mouth   w   our family had
dispersed: my husband to the waiting room   my older brother gone   my mother to
the parking lot to get the car   my younger brother waiting with me in the room

a tech came to move you from the bed to a wheelchair so you could be discharged   once in
the chair, the seizure happened, although it wasn't really a seizure   the relentless shaking
enough to make me think you might die   your eyes were open, conscious, watching it
all unfold as heat infiltrated your body and your nerves could not be quieted

the tech went to find help, left my brother and I alone in the cold room   my brother, 14-years-
old, was just as infiltrated by heat as he cried and yelled into the hallway for a tech a nurse a
doctor anyone to come help our father   shaking   having a seizure   the blood in
his mouth
help him
help us help us help us

and I watched through the glass doors of the room as a doctor behind the check-in counter ate
yogurt and read an article from a magazine and a nurse arranged paperwork in a folder and my
brother cried and yelled hit the wall with his closed fist my husband came and I shoved my
brother into the hallway,

his adolescent muscles baking under my hands as my husband pulled him into a tight embrace
   pinned him against the wall their faces close together my brother calming in his grasp
and all I could think to do in the cold room

was put my hands on my father's shoulders and pray out loud   through chattering teeth and
bloody mouth he said *I can't hear what you're saying*
I said *I'm not talking to you*
and he knew I was praying and I think it scared him to know that I was that afraid   that I
was that terrified and I didn't know how to make the shaking stop so through tears I could barely

speak but asked for the seizure that wasn't quite a seizure to stop *save my father God*
   bring us peace

eventually the shaking stopped   my mother came in   we all stood for hours in the
room waiting for someone to tell us what had happened and a nurse said I was compromising
other patients' privacy by standing in the open doorway of my father's room so I went back
in all of us standing in a circle around him as he was slumped over in the wheelchair and

later in his permanent room a doctor showed us an x-ray of my father's back with the lower
vertebrae exploded into shards the nerves and spine exposed the seizure that brought him to the
hospital in the first place so violent it literally broke his bones made
the aggressive shaking take over his body and they were going to send him home and tell him to
rest   keep up with your meds   this is your life now with epilepsy

INTERVIEW

KRISTIN LAFOLLETTE

What inspired the poem?

When I was almost eighteen, my father was in a serious accident that almost killed him. Years later, he had a violent seizure at work, and the doctor who saw him in the emergency room thought it was a fluke. A short time later, he had another seizure. My mother called me and let me know what happened, and my husband and I drove the hour to the hospital to see him. My brothers were both there (at the time, my younger brother was fourteen and my older brother was twenty-five). This night ended up turning into one of the most difficult experiences of my life. The doctor was going to discharge my father and have him follow-up with another doctor, so my older brother left and my mother went to get the car to pick him up, leaving me, my husband, and my younger brother in the room. The poem is about what happened next, and I really struggled to be able to tell this story any other way than through the stream of consciousness that comes through in the poem. My father began shaking uncontrollably like he was having a seizure, but he was conscious. There were doctors and nurses and techs at the nurses' station and walking the halls, but no one would help. We were actually chastised for going out into the hallway to find help because we were "compromising the privacy of other patients." We found out later that the second seizure literally shattered the lumbar portion of my father's back, so the nerves were exposed. That's what caused the uncontrollable shaking when he was moved from the hospital bed to the wheelchair. And the doctor was just going to send him home.

What was the hardest part about writing it?

I think I find it easier to write about difficult moments in my life because I see writing as a therapeutic process, but this one was a bit more difficult to write. The wounds still feel fresh in some ways, and as I was writing this poem, I kept thinking back to my fourteen-year-old brother calling out for help and just being so upset and confused as to why no one would come help us. While it was difficult to sit and write this, I feel better about it being "on paper." The story is out in the world to be told and shared; it no longer sits alone in the back of my mind.

What came easiest when writing this poem?

Because the event that this poem is about is such a blur in my mind, the easiest part of this poem was writing it as a stream of consciousness. When I think back on that night, everything happened so quickly and I remember the room being so hot and my mind racing as I tried to sort out what to do—how to help my father, my brother. There are moments from that night that stick out more in my mind, but for the most part, the whole thing sort of blurs together, so it only made sense for me to write the poem this way.

Is this poem categorical of your work? Why or why not?

This isn't really the type of work I normally do, but I'm starting to experiment more with hybrid-genre writing. I see myself first and foremost as a poet, but I often explore intersecting poetry with other forms and modes (I'm very interested in the intersections of art and writing, for example). This piece feels like a hybrid of nonfiction and poetry to me, since it's about something that happened to me and my family but is a bit different than a typical piece of prose.

How long have you been writing poetry?

I started out in college as a pre-med major and was almost through my program (studying for the MCAT and getting ready to apply to medical school) when I decided I needed a change. I've been interested in writing my whole life, so I decided to try English (I know, this sounds like a big life change, and it was). During my first creative writing elective as an English major, I fell in love with poetry. There was so much freedom with form, and I appreciated how meticulous and rhetorical poetry was. That was almost ten years ago, and I've been writing poetry ever since (and because of how impactful that first creative writing class was for me, I went on to get an MA in English and creative writing and a PhD in writing studies).

Do you work in any other artistic mediums? If so, how do those other genres inform your poetry?

I consider myself to be a writer, an artist, and a photographer, and my work often blurs the lines of genre. I recently completed a PhD in writing studies, and my dissertation advocated for the use of art in writing. I appreciate the way image and text work together to create altogether new writing/reading/viewing experiences for the author and for the audience. I do a lot of visual poetry and collage work, and I've composed a few full-length projects that use both visual and textual elements. I'm currently working on a memoir-in-poems about growing up in the Midwest in a family of hunters.

Where can readers find more of your work?

I have poetry recently published in or forthcoming from *Spectrum Literary Journal, Noble / Gas Qtrly, SHARK REEF, Epigraph Magazine,* and *Poetry South*. I've also recently had poetry published in the anthologies *Epiphanies and Late Realizations of Love* (*Transcendent Zero Press*) and *America's Emerging Poets 2018: Midwest Region* (*Z Publishing*). I have a piece of flash fiction forthcoming in *Hypertext Magazine*, recently had a piece of nonfiction published in *The Curator*, and have had art/writing hybrid work published recently in *Slippery Elm Literary Journal* and *LossLit*. I have art recently featured in or forthcoming from *Chronically Lit, Orange Blossom Review,* and *Fearsome Critters*.

What drew you to *Driftwood Press*?

I was drawn to *Driftwood Press* because of their openness to hybrid work. Since my work is so often at the intersections of multiple genres, I sometimes have a difficult time finding a home for my work. I appreciate that more and more presses and literary journals and magazines are becoming digital as this tends to open up the possibilities for publishing hybrid work with unique forms and mediums.

The Business of Orange

RIKKI SANTER

was my mother's leather jacket, bold tangerine her private
blood pulse for arming a closet with the triumph of hue.

Now from her protege of color, my front door will command
you like a marmalade portal to a Pantone universe. My life

raft, a love for composites—juicy chemistry of saffron and
tomato saucing up my draperies and rugs. The divine rhythms

of infrared frequencies to harmonize with skies azure—and
mother sang, smiling at me. My father's protective tutelage

at the fruit stand—how to properly read the rind and dodge acid
headed for the eyes. A sudden bloom on my brother's city sidewalk,

umbrellas bursting open pumpkin and blue. Yet my Cara Cara
trees never survived Ohio, year-round sunlight temperamental

at best, but when my husband late at night brings me tea laced
with orange blossom honey, white petals softly light upon my chest.

INTERVIEW

RIKKI SANTER

What inspired the poem?

My mother's flamboyant love for color was one of her greatest lessons for me and to this day, I marvel at the colors in our world. One late afternoon, coming home from a stressful day at work, I plopped myself down on my front stoop and began musing about my orange front door. The rest of the poem seemed to come through as the idea of orange coalesced in my memories.

Is this poem categorical of your work?

A companion poem for this one comes from one of my previous collections and is titled, "Blue." Also, when writing ekphrastic poems in response to artwork, which I often do, I'm always first attuned to color.

What is your favorite line from the poem or the line you are most proud of?

My husband is a painter and his sumptuous minimalist style is all about the luminous quality of hue. The last couplet of the poem is a love note to him and his life's commitment to color.

If you had to narrow it down, what three books have had the most impact on your writing?

This dynamic is fluid for me. I can only answer this question by reporting which three books are on my nightstand right now: *Parole* by Angie Estes; *Map: Collected and Last Poems* by Wisława Szymborska; *Monster: Distortion, Abstraction, and Originality in Contemporary American Poetry (Studies in Modern Poetry)* by Mark Irwin.

Based on your personal experience, what advice would you give to other writers?

Do it your way.

What drew you to *Driftwood Press*?

I've long admired the vibrancy and integrity of its editors. It's an honor for me to have my work included in these pages.

Where can readers find more of your work?

Thanks for asking. Amazon, Goodreads, and my website (www.rikkisanter.com).

ZEROS AND ONES AND OTHER NUMBERS

ALISON LANDES

1. twenty dollars

today I learned how to say
you raped me.

I know the coin-op is an inconvenience but
don't you think red suits you?
the blood of a virgin is in this year. at least

that's what I've heard. please
promise me you won't like this status.

2. fifty minutes

the internet tells me you are an engineer.
in zeros and ones,
my body was a limp sideways cylinder
on your twin extra-long bed

will you carry your daughter
with those arms? please engineer me
a new past. I am not a girl
who codes,
        some days I'm not a girl
at all

3. one person who believes me

the world ends where you get hard to this.
        I begin somewhere else.
don't act like you've read lao tzu. did you really think
you stepped on your own mouth?

the wind tonight
is a screaming woman, banging together
tree limbs with her soprano. I think
I see a spark. she might just
burn us all down.

"IDENTITY SERIES 1" | MAURICIO PAZ VIOLA

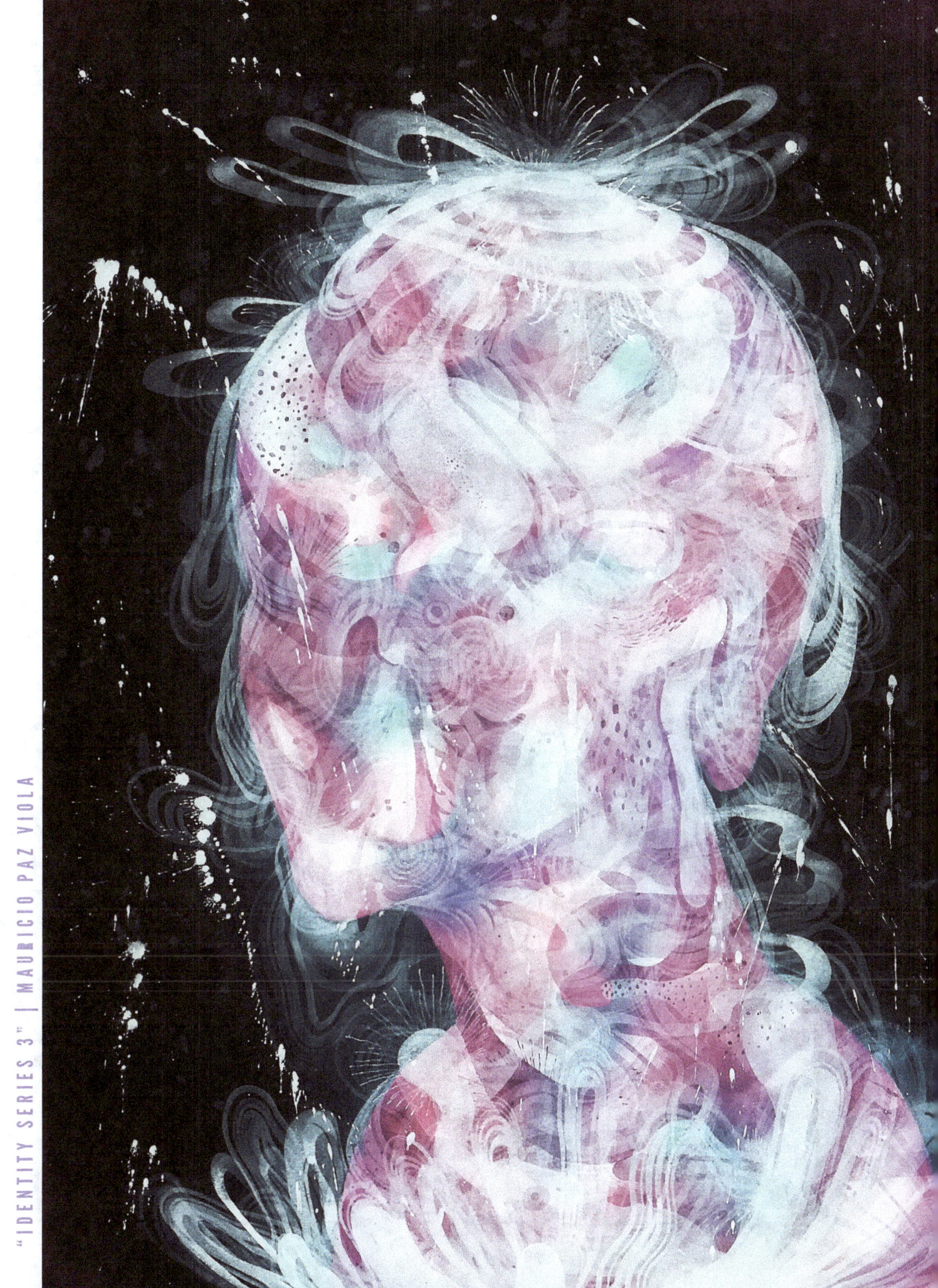

"IDENTITY SERIES 3" | MAURICIO PAZ VIOLA

RIP Scott R. Smith

WHAT?
WHAT THE HELL IS THIS?
THAT? IT'S JUST A LITTLE TEAR.
JUST A LITTLE TEAR? I'M A GHOST, IRIS. THAT'S NOT EVEN FABRIC! IT'S...
WHAT IS IT?
SOUL? HOW DID I RIP MY SOUL?
ALRIGHT, BRIAN, LET'S NOT COMPLETELY—
—HANG ON—

– I THINK I SEE SOMETHING.
THERE'S SOMETHING INSIDE...
INSIDE?
INSIDE WHERE?
...LIKE A PLANT...
...A LITTLE SEEDLING GROWING UNDER YOUR SHEET.
VERY FUNNY.
IT REMINDS ME OF A TOMATO PLANT. DO YOU REMEMBER THOSE?

TOMATO PLANT? IRIS, WE'VE BEEN DEAD FOR THREE CENTURIES AND I'VE SPENT MOST OF THAT TIME IN THIS ATTIC WITH THE DUST.
NOW YOU'RE TELLING ME THAT I'M SOME KIND OF POT? A GARDEN?
THERE'S NO WAY THAT'S GOOD NEWS.
WHAT IF IT...
JUST...
KEEPS...
GROWING?
I'M NOT TELLING YOU ANYTHING-
-EXCEPT WHAT I SEE.
DO YOU WANT ME TO TRY PULLING IT OUT?

WILL IT HURT?
I DON'T KNOW...
...I DON'T THINK SO.
OKAY. JUST DO IT QUICK.
ON THREE. ONE...
TWO...
TWO AND A HALF...

TWO AND TWO THIRDS...
TWO AND THREE QUARTERS...
THREE.
IRIS?
DID YOU DO IT?
IS IT OUT?
YEAH.
I THINK SO.

OW.

YOU FELT THAT?

OH,
I DON'T KNOW.
I WAS PROBABLY JUST... REMEMBERING.

WELL, YOU'RE OKAY NOW.
RIGHT.

HEY–YOU WANT TO GO HAUNTING WITH ME?
IT'LL MAKE YOU FEEL LESS ALIVE.

I DON'T THINK I WANT TO FEEL LESS ALIVE.
I'LL BE DOWNSTAIRS IF YOU NEED ME.
I LOVED YOU.
LOVED YOU TOO.

INTERVIEW

SCOTT SMITH

Welcome back to the pages of *Driftwood*, Scott! Let's start the interview with you catching us up. What's been going on in your comics career since we published *Invasive Studies* in issues 2.2-4.1?

First, it's great to be back in *Driftwood Press* where I have so many happy memories working through *Invasive Studies*! Since then, I've published a comic called "Cup & Socket" in *Barrelhouse Magazine* about a robot talking over the possibility of building its own child. I've also been doing a series of pictures for a middle-grade book I'm writing as well as graphic design for board games.

Looking at this short as compared to *Invasive Studies*, how has your art and approach to storytelling evolved?

Artistically, I'm definitely more comfortable taking risks than I was at the beginning of *Invasive Studies*. I had a lot of fun overlapping greys in this one as the ghost shapes merged. In terms of the story, I hope readers can still recognize my focus on the quiet-but-important conversations that happen behind the scenes in relationships. I'm growing more flexible with symbols as I try out each fantastic lens—aliens, robots, now ghosts.

We've now published both your longform and shortform comics. How does the drafting process differ between the two?

Well, once we got into the swing of things with *Invasive Studies*, it was always a crunch trying to get that next issue together! Tons of great creativity came out of that crunch and I'm so glad I did it, but the drafting process for "RIP" was far more leisurely.

Was the singular use of green against an otherwise stark gray backdrop always intentional? How does working with color change your artistic process?

I wanted to have this natural, otherwise inconspicuous green pop onto the page in an almost a threatening way. In this story, life takes on the normal roll of death, so I wanted to make life feel foreign and intrusive. Adding color, when I don't normally use color, allowed me to do that.

What inspired "RIP"? Tell us more about the origins of this story and whether any aspects of it were inspired by real life.

I started "RIP" not long after hearing that my father was diagnosed with a treatable form of cancer a few years ago. My family has been lucky enough to avoid serious health complications through my childhood and young adult life, so this was a big moment for us. I chose ghosts as symbols of immortality and invulnerability. Their afterlife is assured and secure. The rip disturbs that security. Flipping death to life makes it more approachable for me—and I hope more approachable for my readers—giving me a safer space to consider these ideas.

Tell us a little more about the process of drafting "RIP."

I started sketching a bunch of ghosts until I came up with this asymmetrical, big-eyed version that connected with me—kind of innocent and off kilter. Then I wrote a conversation between the ghosts in dialog format to explore the arc of the conversation. Next was a mess of unintelligible thumbnailing in the sketchbook until the layout started to materialize.

Once that took shape, the project had momentum and the paneling, sketching, inking, scanning, digitizing and finishing rolled along smoothly enough. I'm close to the point where I may start to draw the sketches with my drawing tablet and save myself a lot of work, but I created "RIP" the same way I created *Invasive Studies.*

What was the hardest part of crafting "RIP"?

The hardest single element was trying to draw the rip itself—I got stuck for a long time with that.

What instruments did you use to craft "RIP"?

Pencil first, inked with a #2 round brush, through Photoshop to clean it up, then finished and colored with my drawing tablet in Autodesk Sketchbook.

Who/what are some of your biggest comic inspirations?

Brandon Graham continues to be an artist I just want to look at again and again. I've also spent some time with Quentin Blake's illustrations in the Roald Dahl books recently.

What other mediums have influenced your work? How?

My fiction work of course keeps me sharp in terms of the writing. My work with indie board games keeps me designing and developing my digital drawing skills—I'm looking forward to bringing some new tricks into play for future comics.

Where can our readers find more of your work? Have you been published before?

Driftwood Press 2.2-4.1! You'll find all of *Invasive Studies* along with a ton of other people's great writing. I also have two children's stories forthcoming in *SPIDER* and *Zizzle* magazines this year and my board game "Dungeon Drop" should be on Kickstarter this summer.

What are you working on now?

I'm currently working on a middle-grade novel titled *The Curse Collector*. While I don't have an active comic project, my wife and I recently took in a foster child and I've begun to get some comics ideas around that experience—maybe even a return to the world of *Invasive Studies*?

Is there anything else you'd like to tell us about this work in particular?

Love you, Mom and Dad.

training wheels

by: Ali Viknyanskiy

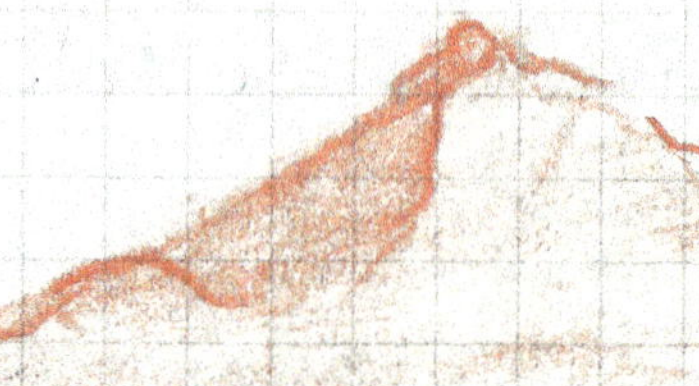

...the snow that once covered Mt. Hood long replaced by a layer of red dust...

Gresham, OR

ZENO, DON'T YOU THINK IT'S PRETTY NEAT THAT WE LIVE NEXT TO A POOL?

WE LIVED IN A COMPLEX WHERE THE POOL WAS FILLED IN WITH GRAVEL, AND MATTIAS, MY YOUNGER BROTHER, LEARNED HOW TO RIDE HIS BIKE GOING IN CIRCLES AROUND IT.

the kidnapped boys made homes in the provided institution-style houses.

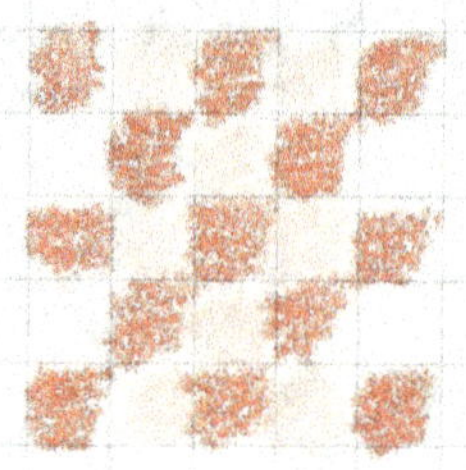

I DON'T THINK THE OTHER BOYS AT SCHOOL HAVE POOLS IN THEIR COMPLEXES.

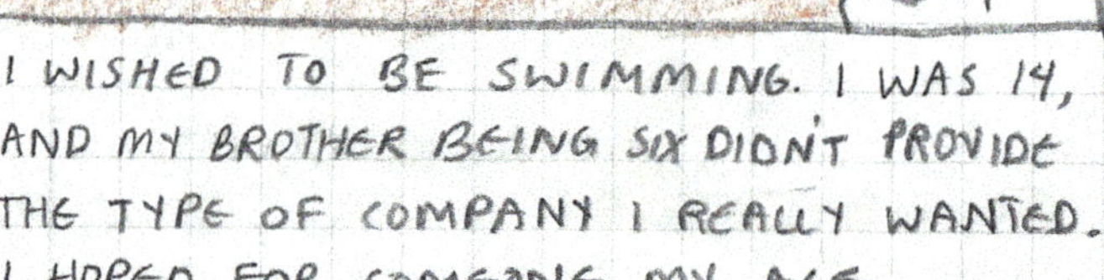

I WISHED TO BE SWIMMING. I WAS 14, AND MY BROTHER BEING SIX DIDN'T PROVIDE THE TYPE OF COMPANY I REALLY WANTED. I HOPED FOR SOMEONE MY AGE.

AIRCRAFTS HAD BEEN SPRINKLING YOUNG BOYS INTO GRESHAM FOR MONTHS POST OUR ARRIVAL, AND BOYS AS YOUNG AS THREE WERE BEING LEFT HERE NOW.

Mom left us at the mall ice-skating rink.

ONCE A MONTH ON A SUNDAY WE WOULD TAKE THE TRAIN TO THE MALL AND SHE WOULD LEAVE US AT THE RINK TO SKATE IN CIRCLES WHILE SHE SHOPPED.

I DON'T REMEMBER WHAT HAPPENED FOR A BIT AFTER. SHE NEVER CAME BACK, AND THEN WE MET MRS. KEY. WE CRIED AND ASKED FOR MOM FOR THE FIRST FEW WEEKS.

I FLIPPED MATTHIAS' BICYCLE UPSIDE-DOWN AND PROPPED IT UP ON ITS HANDLE BARS AND SEAT.

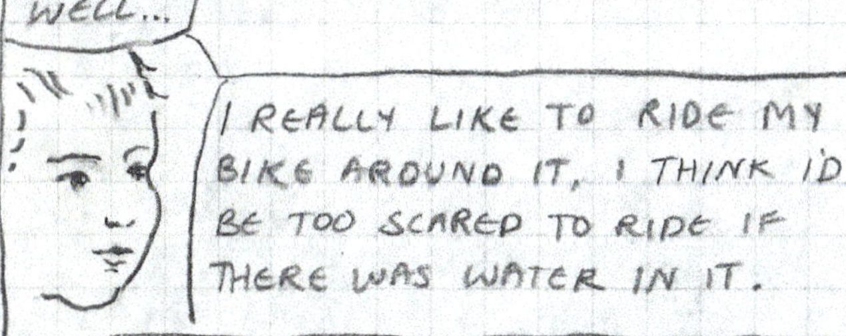

MATTHIAS SLUMPED ON THE DIRT GROUND AND LOOKED UP AT THE SKY. NOT A CLOUD. EMPTY HILLS LINED THE HORIZON AND EMPTINESS WOVE BETWEEN APARTMENT COMPLEXES.

DID HE REMEMBER THE EVERGREENS? OR MOM?

I TOLD MATTHIAS OF THE BOY WHO DROWNED IN THAT POOL BECAUSE ANOTHER BOY HIT HIM WITH A BRICK ON THE HEAD.

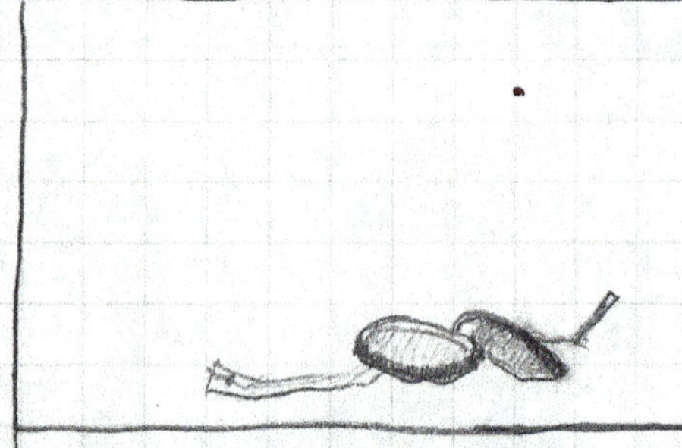

I TOOK THE TRAINING WHEELS OFF. THEY SAT PROPPED AGAINST ONE ANOTHER NEXT TO THE BIKE.

The pool was a grave, not a victory.

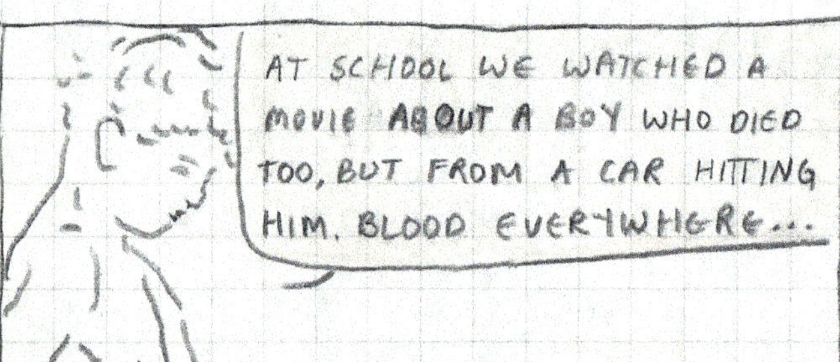

I WORKED SILENTLY. HE DIDN'T GET IT. WE WERE BEING GROOMED TO BE KILLERS, TO NOT FEEL COMPASSION.

OUR TEACHER MRS. KEY SAYS SHE LOVES MOVIES BASED ON REAL STORIES, EVEN IF THEY ARE SAD. SHE SAYS WE SHOULDN'T CRY BECAUSE PUPS DON'T CRY.

I KNEW MRS. KEY WAS HIS FAVORITE TEACHER — SHE WAS ALL HE WOULD TALK ABOUT. SHE WAS ONE OF THE ONLY ADULTS, ONLY FEMALES MATTHIAS CAME IN CONTACT ANYMORE. I WAS THE ONE TO SEE SHE WAS POISONING US.

WHO KNOWS, MAYBE ONE DAY MATTHIAS WILL KILL AND NOT FELL SAD. WE ARE TAUGHT HOW TO WRAP OUR HANDS AROUND OUR FAVORITE ANIMAL'S THROAT UNTIL THEIR EYES ROLL BACK AND THEY STOP STRUGGLING.

MATTHIAS KILLED A FOX CUB. I HEAR ITS SCREAMS EACH TIME THE BIKE'S BRAKES SQUEAK.

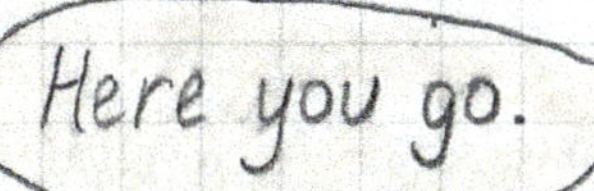

MATTHIAS EAGERLY GRABBED THE HANDLE BARS AND WALKED THE BIKE BACK TO THE EDGE OF THE POOL. I WATCHED HIM CAUTIOUSLY MOUNT THE BICYCLE AND RESUME HIS SLOW WOBBLY CIRCLES AROUND THE POOL, A CLOUD OF DUST BRUSHING HIS FOOT EACH TIME HE'D STEADY HIMSELF.

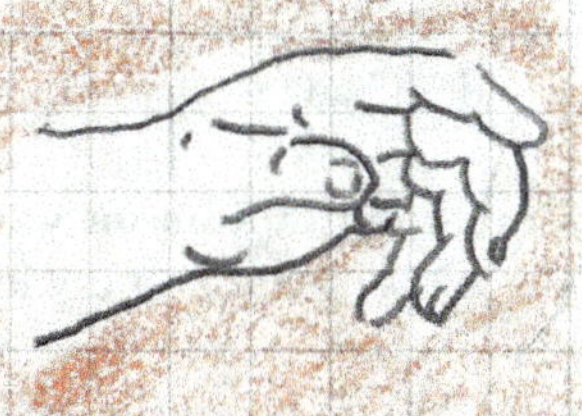

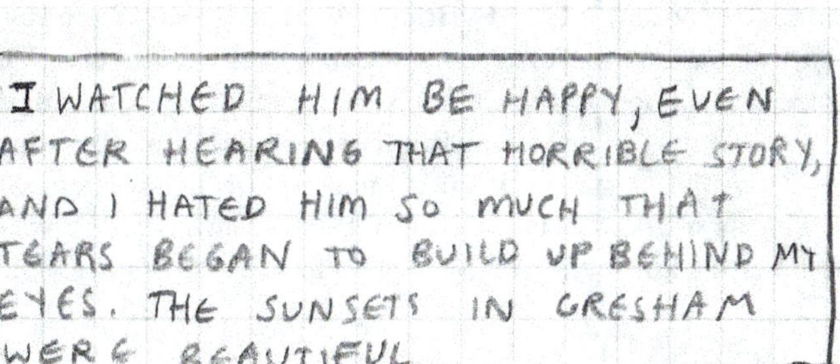

End.

INTERVIEW

ALI VIKNYANSKIY

Despite comics being a very visual medium, you made the decision to tell much of the story through text-based narration. Could you talk about that decision and what it adds to the tone of the story?

"Training Wheels" is a look inside a memory in the form of a journal entry. The text is essentially Zeno's thoughts and the images are visual memories that supplement his inner monologue.

This short work explores a small facet of what seems to be a much larger fictional work. How do you tackle such different worlds in the short story format? Is this meant also to be part of a larger collection?

Though there is a greater story that could be told, this story was always meant to be just a little nugget of dystopia. It was a goal of mine from the beginning to tell a story of a different world in only a few pages without leaving the reader frustrated.

The comic has an interesting structure; the backstory is told through text boxes while a more specific scene is shown with both images and text. How'd you land on this structure?

I chose this structure to help distinguish between what is being recollected from long ago and what is being recollected from the more recent interaction between the two brothers. Memories can be all over the place, bouncing from one and leading into another, and this structure helps organize everything for the reader a bit.

What inspired "Training Wheels"? Tell us more about the origins of this story and whether any aspects of it were inspired by real life.

I wanted to write about something that I feared, and certain things people do can be very scary. That is how I landed on conveying a post-apocalyptic totalitarian environment. Many of the lighter aspects are based on my own childhood growing up in Gresham. My older brother taught me to ride my bike going in circles around a gravel-filled pool. Our mother used to leave us at the skating rink on Sundays and I would wonder if anyone would want to kidnap us.

Could you talk about your use of colors in this piece? Why did you decide on grid paper?

The color choice was partially based on the pencils I had on hand. I picked out two colors that went well with the tone of the story—pink for the dust and the sunsets, blue for the somberness and the pool. The grid paper added an extra layer of depth while tying the colors together.

How did "Training Wheels" change from its first draft?

I spent a lot of time revising the story. Though this story was meant to be short from the very beginning, part of the challenge was to still include adequate context. I very carefully picked out each and every sentence that is included in this comic.

Handwritten lettering is used in many of our favorite comics and graphic novels. What do you think it adds to the reading experience? Some of the wording is smudged. Was this intentional?

I am a huge fan of hand-lettering as well—it adds a level of honesty and personality, and it helps the reader connect to the story's voice on a more intimate level. The smudges, grit, and mistakes were left intentionally for that reason too. Its raw! It fits this story.

The paneling in "Training Wheels" is unconventional. Could you talk about the decisions that went in to shaping the pages?

I am depicting a memory through this piece, and memories can weasel out all over the place, yet usually return to the main subject after a while. I tried to mimic that pattern in the paneling. However, I did keep conventional "rules" in mind, like writing from left to right, top to bottom, but with everything else I went into a bit of an euphoric madness. I put images and text where they made sense and how they would have flowed through Zeno's head, as long as each page was visually balanced at the end.

What instruments did you use to craft "Training Wheels"?

Crafting the comic itself was very simple. Once the story was written, I sat down with three pencils and my own personal journal and wrote, drew, and colored it all in one go. I then tore the pages out of my journal and scanned them, leaving in all the grit. It is a grim story, and I wanted it to look a bit like that too.

Who/what are some of your biggest comic inspirations?

I love the *Naughty Pete* comics by Charles Forbell. His line work and strip layouts are spot on. *The Hokusai Manga* (a collection of Katsushika Hokusai's illustrations) is also absolutely lovely—the color palette and the handling of facial and body expression is perfect. Arsene Schrauwen is also a great inspiration.

What other mediums have influenced your work? How?

Printmaking is a huge influence on my work. The emphasis on line work which then layered over color and again layered on top of the printing surface. I find myself thinking of layers in everything that I create.

Where can our readers find more of your work? Have you been published before?

I have been published for the first time earlier this year! My graphic memoir, *Collector*, was published in *Aquifer: The Florida Review Online* in February. More of my work can be found on my website (shakeylittlehands.com), and I occasionally post illustrations on my personal Instagram (@hey.grandma).

For any of our readers who are aspiring artists, what is one piece of advice you wished someone would have told you when you started drawing comics?

Your comics don't have to be action-packed and full of superheros and villains if you don't want them to be. You are the ruler of what you create!

What are you working on now?

I currently have two long-form pieces in the works. One is about a little cow's sad search for love and connection, and the other is my father's story. Both are playful and funny with bitterness running through the background.

What drew you to *Driftwood Press*?

What drew me to *Driftwood Press* was your curation and efforts which support artists' unique explorations and creativity. I appreciate the intentionality that is clearly involved in your publications.

Goodbye, Samantha.

by

Nick St. John

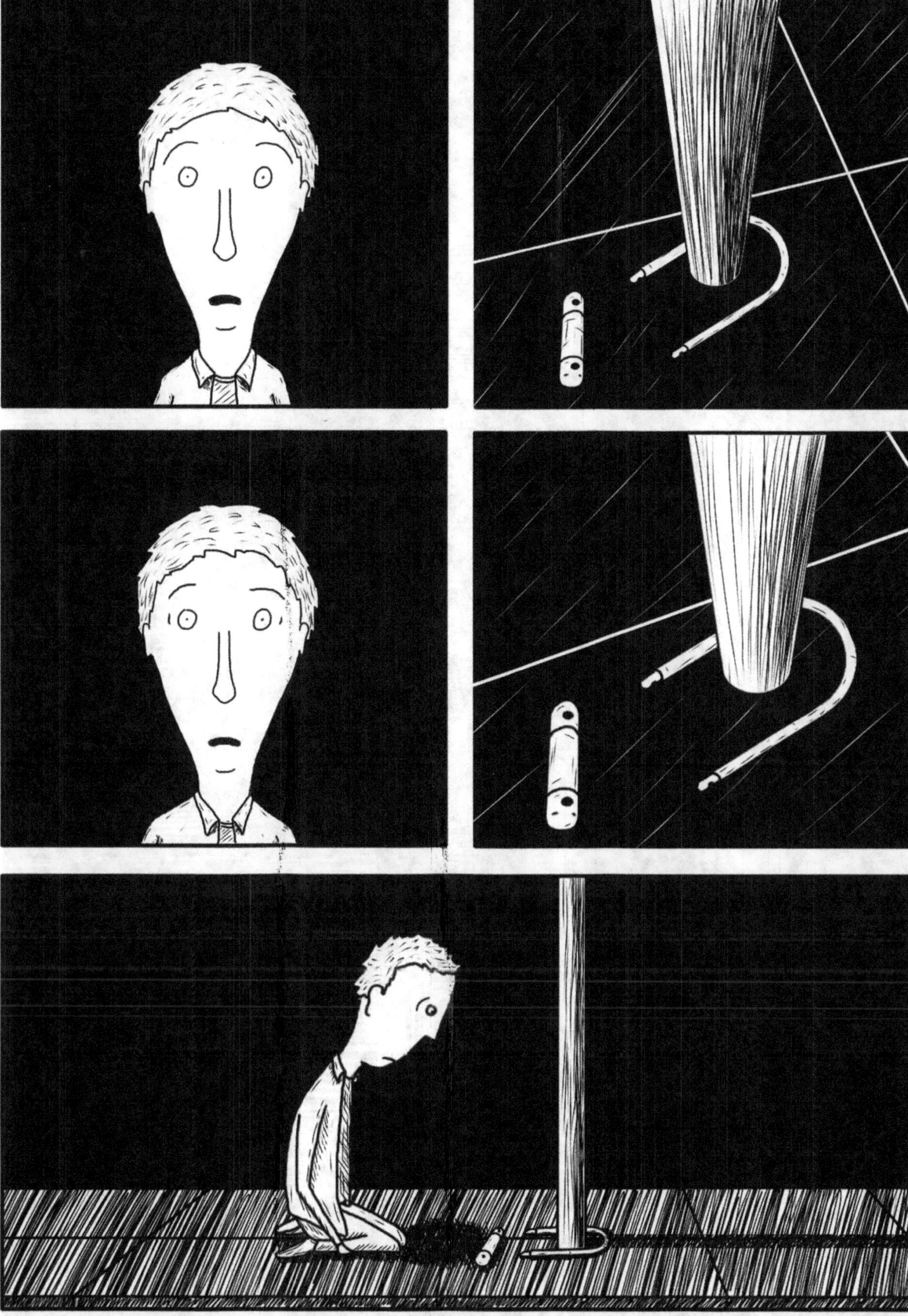

INTERVIEW

NICK ST. JOHN

This comic clearly inhabits a surrealist, comedic space. Is this categorical of your work?

I guess it is, yeah. But I never really set out to do that. A lot of my work, including this piece, is driven by a reluctance to accept reality as it's presented. As far as comedy goes, I find that a lot of what I try to present as tragic people find funny and vice-versa, which is okay with me. I've always enjoyed blending the line between the two. I guess I feel like that's a better representation of real life. Few things are ever purely funny or tragic.

We love the stark contrasts of black and white coloring in this comic. Were other colors ever considered? What, in your mind, are the strengths behind black and white artwork?

I'd love to pretend this was a deeply thought-out artistic choice. I do think it works really well for this comic, but the truth is that I'm just terrible at working with color, so I generally don't do it.

We love the second page's establishing shot. Often in film and comics, the establishing shot is given before the close-up, but here it appears after—almost to a comedic effect. Could you talk about that decision to zoom out rather than zoom in?

Oh man, I love this kind of question. I don't think it ever even occurred to me to do it any other way. Sometimes I spend days rearranging the words and images in a comic, trying to achieve a certain effect, but this one kind of came to me all at once, fully formed. Looking at it now, though, I feel like it works because the whole comic is an expansion. It begins with the intimacy of loss and pain, of a terrible new reality dawning, then expands to encompass the setting of this sadness. There is the sinking reality that one now must walk home across this huge and cruel city which, like our own loss, can so easily fool us into thinking it is the entire world. And finally the last expansion to a world that is beautiful and vast and infinitely full of possibility. So much bigger than that city or the one shitty night when your bike got stolen. Yeah.

What were some of the difficulties faced when drawing this comic—especially the two pages that lack panels?

As I mentioned, and I swear I'm not just trying to be charmingly self-effacing here, I really don't know what I'm doing as an illustrator. People often compliment me on my crude and simplistic art style. I rarely have the heart to tell them that's actually the best human face I can draw. So pretty much the whole comic was drawn with tremendous difficulty, especially the last page. I kind of put off thinking about it until the rest was already done, and then looking at my script notes I was like, "you've got to be kidding me. There's no way I can draw that." I think I spent a full day just trying to figure out what a bike looks like riding away. That's the fun challenge of working in comics for me, though. With every piece I get just a little better at it.

On page two, someone is looking at the protagonist from above. If you had to give backstory to this mysterious silhouette, what would it be?

I would never! That figure exists entirely to give you, the reader, the joy of providing your own backstory.

If comedy relies, as they say, on expectations, your piece certainly stands as evidence. Do you have any tips for comedy writers?

I don't really. Sorry comedy writers. You are on your own.

So, uh, where did the bike go?

Well, that's the whole question here, isn't it? Obviously the go-to assumption would be that the bike got stolen because somebody wound up at the bar a lot longer than intended or else they wouldn't have left it locked up on a poorly-lit side street well into the nefarious hours of night. I also think its possible that it just got fed up with being ridden in an endless triangle (home-work-bar-home) every day and ran away to explore the desert roads of Nevada by moonlight. Seeing as we will never know for sure, I choose to believe in the possibility that is less depressing.

How did "Goodbye, Samantha" change from its first draft?

I'm flattered that you believe I do multiple drafts of these things.

Tell us a little more about the process of drafting "Goodbye, Samantha."

This was an unusual comic for me as my process almost always begins with words. I'll generally have the text of a comic finished before I begin to think seriously about the images. This was conceived as images from the very beginning and, as I mentioned earlier, it kind of came to me all at once. From there it was just a question of getting the right feel with the pacing of the frames and making everything fit onto the page in a way I liked. There's always a bit of compromise in that process, but It's important to me that each page begins and ends like a sentence so that the layout becomes part of the structure of the whole thing.

What instruments did you use to craft "Goodbye, Samantha"?

I did this piece in ink on paper, then scanned it and gave it a digital polish to correct a few mistakes and fill in the large black areas and white highlights which is otherwise super tedious.

Who/what are some of your biggest comic inspirations?

I think the first comic I ever read was Sam Keith's *The Maxx*, which I still think is brilliant, but it was artists like Dan Clowes, Art Spiegleman, and Ben Katchor whose work first showed me the range of things that can be done with comics. At the time I was mostly working on prose fiction and suffering the classic "everything has been done before" syndrome. Discovering this relatively new medium and the tremendous, largely unexplored potential of synthesizing words and images was incredibly liberating. To me there are few things as inspiring as someone telling a story in a way you've never seen before.

Where can our readers find more of your work? Have you been published before?

I've been published in a whole bunch of literary magazines over the years. The best place to see more of my work is my website (nickstjohn.net).

What are you working on now?

For the moment I've stood up from the drawing table and stretched my legs a bit. Currently, I live on some land in the mountains where I run a peach orchard and restore old sailboats. Kind of doing a surf and turf sort of thing. I expect some evening soon the urge to make comics will strike me again. Meanwhile, the world remains full of other wonderful things to do with one's time.

CONTRIBUTORS

SUSAN JARDANEH holds an MFA from the University of North Carolina at Greensboro. She's been published in *The Southern Review, Carve, The Berkeley Review*, and other magazines.

JOE TOTTEN has been writing professionally for twenty years as an advertising copywriter. "The Starling Killers" is his first short story publication.

ZACHARY WILLIAMS is a writer and multidisciplinary artist from Augusta, Georgia. He currently resides in Mississippi, where he is a PhD candidate in poetry at Southern Miss's Center for Writers. His poetry has appeared in *The Axe Factory, FORTH Magazine*, and *Mush/Mum*.

ALBERT LEE is a junior at Macalester College in Saint Paul, Minnesota. His writing is inspired by larger questions about postmemory, transindividuality, Asiafuturism, and Cardi B. As his mother once said, "You need less Cardi B and more Cardi O."

RAINIE OET is a queer nonbinary writer and game designer. They are the author of three books: *Porcupine in Freefall* (winner of the *Bright Hill Press* Poetry Book Competition, 2019), *Inside Ball Lightning* (*SEMO Press*, 2020), and *Glorious Veils of Diane* (*Carnegie Mellon University Press*, 2021). They have an MFA in Poetry from Syracuse University, where they received the Shirley Jackson Prize in Fiction. Read more on their website (rainieoet.com).

SHERRI LEVINE lives in Portland, Oregon where she teaches English to immigrant and refugee students. Her work has been published in *The Timberline Review, Williwaw Journal, Verseweavers*, and *The Sun Magazine*. She won First Prize in the Oregon Poetry Association's Contest (2017). Sherri served as Poetry Editor for *VoiceCatcher: A Journal of Women's Voices & Vision*. Her debut chapbook, *In These Voices*, was published by *The Poetry Box*. You can find more on her website (sherrilevine.com).

LAWRENCE LORRAINE MULLEN is a non-binary poet who holds an MFA in Poetry and is currently a PhD candidate at The State University of New York at Buffalo. They have been published in *Maudlin House, Meow Meow Pow Pow, Ghost City Review, Crab Fat,* and *GTK Creative*. They are also a founding editor of *Harvest Apothecary Review*. You can find them on Twitter and Instagram (@ prince_yikes).

STEPHEN HUNDLEY's work has appeared or is forthcoming in *Notre Dame Review, Carve, Permafrost,* and other journals. He serves as the fiction editor for *The Swamp* and is a Richard Ford Fellow at the University of Mississippi. Some of his work can be viewed on his website (stephenhundley.org).

AMY TROTTER is a poet and MFA candidate at American University. She is an Alabama native currently living, writing, working, and mothering in the suburbs of D.C. with her two children and husband. Her work has appeared in *The Potomac Review, Obsidian, Mezzo Cammin,* and *The American Journal of Poetry*.

SARAH ANDERSON's poems have appeared most recently in *December Magazine, Off the Coast,* and *The Hunger Journal*. Recently, one of her poems was a finalist in a contest (the James Hearst Poetry Contest by *North American Review*). She earned an MFA from the Program for Writers at Warren Wilson College in 2011, and she's a high school English teacher and a mother of two. On her property in New Hampshire, she owns and operates a venue called "The Word Barn," a space for writers and musicians.

KRISTIN LAFOLLETTE is a PhD candidate at Bowling Green State University and is a writer, artist, and photographer. Her work was featured in the anthology *Ohio's Best Emerging Poets* (*Z Publishing*, 2017), and she is the author of the chapbook *Body Parts* (*GFT Press*, 2018). She currently lives in northwest Ohio. You can visit her on Twitter (@k_lafollette03) or on her website (kristinlafollette.com).

RIKKI SANTER's poetry has appeared in numerous publications, including *Ms. Magazine, Poetry East, Margie, The Journal of American Poetry, Hotel Amerika, Crab Orchard Review, Grimm, Slipstream* and *The Main Street Rag*. Her work has received many honors, including four Pushcart and three Ohioana book award nominations as well as a fellowship from the National Endowment for the Humanities. Her seventh collection, *In Pearl Broth*, will be published this spring by *Stubborn Mule Press*. You can find more information about her on her website (www.rikkisanter.com).

ALISON LANDES is a women's health nurse and cat mom living in San Francisco. She writes on the themes of trauma, womanhood, and witchery.

ALEXANDER LANDERMAN is currently working as a freelance artist spending his summer traveling across the United States as a resident artist.

MAURICIO PAZ VIOLA embarked on his artistic journey early in life. Dabbling in plastic art since seven, he has participated in various art competitions in his native Uruguay and abroad. At fourteen, Paz Viola began to participate in group shows and individual shows nationally and internationally in galleries and museums in Uruguay, Argentina, Chile, United States, Italy, among others.

SCOTT SMITH is a writer, comics artist, and tabletop game designer living in Groton, MA. He has a children's story forthcoming in *SPIDER Magazine*, recently published a comic in *Barrelhouse Magazine*, and won Game Crafter's "Game Pieces Only" contest in 2018. You can find more of his work on his website (www.invasivestudies.com).

ALINA VIKNYANSKIY is a writer and cartoonist currently based in Springfield, Missouri. Her work ranges from comics and digital design to conceptual collages, photo art direction, and textile soft sculpture. She recently had a comic published in *Aquifer: The Florida Review Online*. You can follow her on Instagram (@hey.grandma) or on her website (shakeylittlehands.com).

NICK ST. JOHN has been creating graphic lit for about ten years and has been published in *The Best American Non-required Reading, Booth, December, The Black Warrior Review, Iron Horse Review,* and other publications that escape my memory right now. One of his pieces, in pirated form, also occupied the front page of Reddit for several days. He's spent most of the last decade wandering aimlessly about the globe and has most recently settled for a moment on an organic peach farm in California.